RAMEN

RAMEN

50 classic ramen and Asian noodle soups

HEATHER WHINNEY

LORENZ BOOKS

Contents

What is ramen?

In its simplest form, ramen is a delicious mix of wheat noodles, a tasty broth and various carefully selected toppings. That sounds simple enough, but the variations are endless, both within Japan and in fusion form elsewhere. In Japan alone, for instance, the broth can be rich or light, opaque or cloudy, while the toppings range from the chatsu pork typical of Hakata ramen and the pork curry ramen found in Muroran, or ones that feature intensely umami beef, to lighter tofu and vegetable toppings.

In essence, the dish comprises a flavourful base stock made from chicken, pork or vegetables, or dashi (stock made from kombu seaweed and dried fish flakes); a tare, which is the key flavouring element and is defined by the inclusion of shio (salt), shoyu (soy) or miso, in various combinations and often accompanied by other flavourings such as garlic, ginger or chilli; the noodles, which should be wheat-based but the thickness of which can vary; and a range of additional ingredients or toppings.

Within these broad parameters there is much scope for experimentation, although true ramen chefs take great care to produce perfectly balanced dishes rather than simply combining elements on a whim. In this book, we have included a mixture of classic ramen dishes and also some twists and variations, to ring the changes. While a few of these recipes are not strictly authentic, part of the beauty of ramen is its versatility and, given that it is a dish that itself has a complex history of adaptation and mixed lineage, it seems fitting that modern recipe writers can try out new ideas and expand the culinary repertoire of tasty noodle-based soups to enjoy.

below Flavouring or 'tare' staples used in ramen are (clockwise from top) rice vinegar, sesame oil, miso, rice wine or mirin, and soy sauce.

The tangled history of ramen

Generally associated with Japanese cooking and now ubiquitous worldwide in a multitude of variations and formats, the dish now called ramen in fact originated in China and is thought to have only crossed the border to Japan during the early 20th century, although its history is not altogether clear.

What we do know is that at some point around the turn of the 20th century Chinese cooks introduced a new type of wheat noodle, called 'shina soba' ('China noodle'), to Japan. The key difference between classic Japanese noodles such as udon and these newcomers was the use of kansui, a sodium-carbonate mineral water, in their making. The term shina soba was used for the next 30-odd years, but in the aftermath of the Second World War, when the term shina became a racial slur, the noodles were renamed 'chūka soba'. A few years later, however, in 1958, Nissin Foods produced the first packaged instant version of the noodles, which they called 'Chikin Ramen', and the term 'ramen' – a portmanteau word consisting of the Chinese 'la' ('pull') and 'mian' ('noodle') – stuck.

Yet the origin of the noodles themselves are only part of the story, since ramen dishes are as much, if not more, about the flavoured broth and carefully selected toppings. How and why this combination of elements came together is not definitively recorded, but it seems likely that a predecessor was a Chinese dish called laa-mien, which consists of hand-made noodles in a light chicken broth, albeit without any toppings. This could have been introduced to Japanese port cities such as Yokohama, and gone on to inspire the pushcart vendors who soon afterwards were to be found selling ramen as we know it in Tokyo. An alternative theory is that the same Chinese dish provided a customs agent in Yokohama named Ozaki Kenichi with the idea of opening a ramen store called Rai-Rai Ken in Tokyo. His version of the dish featured toppings, as well as the all-important seasoning base for the broth that is a defining feature of the dish today, so it seems likely that his restaurant was at least partially involved with ramen's history.

Whatever its origins, this combination of noodles, broth and toppings proved incredibly popular. Quick, cheap, sustaining and nutritious, ramen was not only a very efficient way of feeding hungry workers – the stock pot could be left boiling away all day, so it was just a matter of swiftly cooking and combining the other elements to order as required – but it was also viewed, along with other foreign foods, as being more healthy and nourishing than traditional Japanese dishes since it contained more calories, fat and protein. Little wonder, then, that ramen vendors and specialist stores soon cropped up all over the place, giving rise to all sorts of regional

above There are many different types of ramen noodles: some are flat, some are wavy, and they come in varying thicknesses.

above Ramen toppings can be whatever ingredients you favour; this winning combination of flash-cooked squid and prawn is infused with the heat of fresh chilli.

variations and refinements in terms of the seasonings and toppings.

The start of the Second World War, and the rationing and food scarcity that this caused, put a stop to the craze, and for nearly a decade the country went hungry and ramen almost disappeared as people stopped dining out. The end of the war, however, soon saw the resurgence of street food, especially dishes made with wheat, such as gyoza (dumplings), yakisoba (fried wheat noodles), okonomiyaki (savoury pancake), and ramen. The revival of these dishes was in part due to the fact that rice was hard to come by during the period of American occupation after the end of the war, whereas wheat was imported from the USA. This shift in favour of wheat-based produce – helped along by government promotion that backed this 'healthy' Western approach to diet – was also evident in the new custom of eating bread, a habit that continues to this day.

In the decades that followed, Japan's economy boomed, and ramen, now bestowed with an almost-mythical status as one of the dishes that had stopped the population from starving, boomed with it. As the country grew, construction workers flocked to cities to earn a living on the vast building sites, and ramen became the ideal food to fuel their endeavours. This, along with the popularity of other 'stamina' wheat-based foods, caused the nation's palate to change, and students and young people, raised on a diet high in wheat and meat relative to that of their predecessors, gradually helped to transform ramen's image from being street food for the poor and labourers, to something you went out to eat at a speciality restaurant, called a ramen-ya.

Since the 1980s, ramen in Japan has been mostly sold at these restaurants (or in instant pot form, but that's another story) rather than by street food vendors, and is consumed by often-fanatical fans called rāmen gyōretsu who are happy to queue for hours outside a sought-after establishment, and endlessly discuss the merits of regional variations. These foodies, with their appetite for both the dish itself and the rhetoric that surrounds it, have helped to elevate ramen cooks to stardom, and the dish is now embraced as being Japanese, rather than a Chinese import.

What's more, as it has become increasingly clear that some aspects of the Western diet are in fact distinctly unhealthy, ramen and other Eastern foods are feted as a healthier option. This, coupled with ramen's image as being wholesome and comforting while at the same time artisanal and a bit hip, has helped to whet the global appetite for the dish, and it has become a staple food in some form or another for millions of people.

below Small mobile food carts serve top-quality ramen bowls to those lucky enough to find them, in Tokyo and further afield.

The stock (base)

Ramen is all about the broth, the simmered stock that is the starting point to the dish, and to which the tare is later added, and the toppings. It is usually made from pork or chicken, or a dashi stock that is made with kombu and smoked bonito or skipjack flakes. A double stock is popular, where two stocks are combined such as chicken and pork, for a more complex flavour.

It is definitely worth making your own stock, and you can make a bulk in advance to portion up and freeze, but you can of course buy a decent ready-made fresh stock or, at a push, use a good-quality stock/bouillon cube. Whichever you choose, taste the stock and reduce it down by simmering if it tastes a bit insipid.

Pork stock

This takes a while to cook but very little preparation is required, though you may need to order the ingredients from your butcher. Plan to make the stock at least a couple of days before you make your ramen. It will sit in the fridge in an airtight container for up to 3 days or you can freeze it for up to 3 months. As you simmer the broth it will start to turn from clear to a milky colour.

4 pig trotters, washed well
1.2kg/2½ lb pork bones, washed well
handful of chicken wings
500g/1lb pork back fat
2 onions, peeled and roughly chopped
4 carrots, roughly chopped

1 Put the pig trotters and pork bones in a large pan, cover with water and bring to the boil. Drain and rinse well with cold water.
2 Put all the ingredients in a large pan and cover with cold water. Bring to a rolling boil and skim away any scum that comes to the surface. The scum should stop after about half an hour.
3 You can now reduce the heat to a low simmer. Put the lid on and cook for 5–6 hours, topping up with water as needed to cover the bones. Over time, the stock will start to change colour and become pale and milky; this is the collagen being released from the bones into the stock.
4 Strain the stock into a large bowl and leave to cool. Skim off any fat that rises to the surface. The stock can be refrigerated, covered, for 2–3 days, or frozen for up to 1 month.
Cook's tip: Wash the pork trotters and bones really well to remove any blood or dirt. You could leave them soaking in water overnight before using, then rinse them well.

Chicken stock

This is a clearer and lighter stock than the pork one, and is not as rich or gelatinous, which makes it ideal for less heavy ramen dishes. It also takes less time to make than the pork stock, but it is still worth cooking it the day before so that it can cool. The chicken meat can be stripped from the carcass and served or stored separately.

1 chicken (preferably free-range), or use the bones and skin from a cooked chicken carcass
3 carrots, roughly chopped
2 leeks, roughly chopped
bunch of spring onions/scallions, roughly chopped
pinch of black peppercorns

1 Put all the ingredients in a large pan and cover with water. Bring to the boil then skim away any scum that comes to the surface as it cooks.
2 Cover and cook on a medium simmer for 2–3 hours. Insert a sharp knife into the chicken thigh; if the juices run clear, it is cooked.
3 Lift out the chicken and transfer it to a dish (to use separately).
4 Strain everything left in the pan into a large bowl. Cover, and put in the fridge once cool. Skim away any fat that has formed on the surface of the stock. The stock can be refrigerated, covered, for 2–3 days, or frozen for up to 1 month.

Vegetable stock

The best way to make vegetable stock is simply to collect offcuts and scraps of vegetables over a few days, and then to boil them up. The vegetables listed here are merely a guide; use what you have, just avoid those that go slimy when cooked, such as soft leaves, cucumber and similar. The addition of ginger, garlic and seaweed imbues the stock with Japanese flavours, ideal for ramen.

about 500g/1lb chopped vegetables, or vegetable scraps, such as carrot, turnip or parsnip tops, onion skins, broccoli or cauliflower stalks, the green tops of leeks and spring onions/ scallions, celery leaves and mushroom stalks
a thumb-sized piece of fresh ginger
2 garlic cloves
a sheet of nori or kombu (if you have some)

1 Give all the vegetables a good wash and check them over.
2 Place everything in a large pan and cover with cold water. Bring to a boil and simmer for about 45 minutes, skimming off any scum that rises to the surface. For more concentrated stock, simmer for longer.
3 Strain the stock into a large bowl and leave to cool. The stock can be refrigerated, covered, for 2–3 days, or frozen.

Kombu dashi stock

This classic Japanese stock is a combination of kombu seaweed and kezuri-bushi, which is dried and smoked (sometimes fermented) tuna flakes. This stock is light and clear but has a rich umami taste from the sea vegetable and makes the perfect light broth base for a ramen dish.

about 25g/1oz kombu
pinch of kezuri-bushi

1 Make a few cuts in the kombu, then put it in a large bowl, cover with water and leave it to soak for an hour.

2 Drain the kombu and put it and the kezuri-bushi in a large pan and cover with about 750ml/1¼ pints/3 cups cold water.

3 Heat gently over a low heat and as soon as the water starts to boil, remove the kombu. This is important, or else the stock will taste bitter. Continue to simmer the stock for about 20 minutes, until it has reduced a little.

4 Remove the stock from the heat and strain it into a large bowl and leave it to cool. The stock can be refrigerated, covered, for 2–3 days, or frozen for up to 1 month.

Cook's tip: If you are short of time, you could use freeze-dried dashi granules called dashi-no-moto, which can be used to make a quick dashi.

The tare (flavourings)

The tare is the element that will transform a simple stock into a delicious broth from which to slurp the noodles. A ramen dish is often categorised into three major flavours: shio (salt), shoyu (soy sauce) and miso, the paste of fermented grains and soybeans. This flavour refers to the primary tare, but they can be used in combination, and many more ingredients can be added.

For the home cook it is easy to mix up a tare with a flavour profile that suits you and then to add it to your stock. It's all about balance – aiming for sweet, spicy, salty or sour. A good place to start is to create a mix of soy sauce and mirin (rice wine) and then to add other ingredients to taste. As a general guide, if you want a cleaner, pure taste, opt for a pinch of salt; for extra umami punch, choose soy sauce; or for more pungency and bolder texture, choose miso.

There are many different types of soy sauce (shoyu), but for ramen the most commonly used one in Japan is called koikuchi, which is just regular dark soy sauce. There are also several types of miso, and the flavour varies according to brand, but as a general rule of thumb, white miso (shiro) is mild and sweet in taste; yellow miso (saikyo) is slightly stronger; and red miso (aka) has the strongest, saltiest flavour. You need less red miso than the other types, and you should use it more carefully, tasting as you add it.

opposite Useful storecupboard ingredients for ramens include white and black rice vinegars, soy sauces, mirin or rice wine, and sake.

Types of noodles

There are hundreds of types of noodles in Japan: fresh, dried, flat, wavy, wide, narrow, thick, fine. What the ones used for ramen have in common is that they are made with wheat flour rather than rice, and traditionally include kansui – the all-important alkaline mixture that gives them a chewy texture and yellow colour. Noodles are picked for a particular ramen dish for their ability to hold the broth and their texture, rather like an Italian chef would choose a particular pasta to suit a sauce. For the home cook, it is down to personal choice. The only rule is: never serve them mushy! The recipes in this book mainly feature fresh ramen noodles. You can swap in dried noodles, but reduce the quantity by one-third and increase the cooking time according to the packet instructions.

How to make noodles

Making traditional hand-pulled ramen noodles is an art that takes many years of practice to perfect. It is usually best just to buy good-quality ones, especially since one of the joys of ramen dishes is their speed. However, if you do want to have a go at making noodles, this recipe creates softer-textured but slightly thicker noodles that taste wonderful and can be made using a rolling pin and knife, although a pasta machine is helpful if you have one. You can use an egg instead of kansui but it won't give quite the same colour, tang and texture.

5ml/1 tsp kansui powder or liquid, or 1 beaten egg
100ml/3½fl oz/scant ½ cup water, or as needed
275g/10oz/2 cups bread or plain (all-purpose) flour

1 Mix the kansui into the water – use the water gradually to judge the amount you need, it should be quite a dry dough. Put the flour in a bowl and make a well in the middle. Pour in the liquid and mix together into a ball.
2 Knead the dough on a floured surface for 5–10 minutes. If you can, rest the dough in the fridge for several hours.
3 Flour the dough ball and place it between two sheets of clear film or plastic wrap, or on a floured surface. Roll out the dough as thinly as possible with a rolling pin. You can do this in batches.
4 If you have a pasta machine, run the dough through this several times to make it as thin as possible.
5 Cut the dough into fine strips and hang it on skewers or a rolling pin suspended between two items of a similar height (or over a container such as a bread bin) and leave it to dry for at least 15 minutes. You could also use the spaghetti attachment on your pasta machine and then hang the noodles to dry.
6 To cook, put the noodles into a pan of rapidly boiling water and cook for about 2–3 minutes, until tender but not disintegrating.

Fresh ramen noodles (left) These are made with a mixture of strong wheat flour, kansui and sometimes egg to help with the elasticity.

Somen noodles (left) Sold in bundles, these very fine white Japanese wheat noodles are perfect in lighter ramens and fish broths.

Instant noodles (left) Crinkled into a brick shape, instant dried noodles can be found in Asian stores – just discard the flavour sachet. They need to be reconstituted in hot water before being added to the broth.

Soba noodles (above) Made from buckwheat, these have a slightly nutty flavour and are a wholesome option in a vegetable ramen.

Udon noodles (left) These flat white wheat noodles have a lovely slippery texture, perfect for slurping from a bowl of ramen.

Long-life fine noodles (below) These long, fine noodles may need to be cut before they are used. They are delicious to slurp and soak up broth.

Dried ramen noodles (below) These take less time to reconstitute than the brick-style instant noodle. They have plenty of bounce and can be added to any broth.

The toppings

above Pork is the most typical meat used in ramen, and the fattier cuts such as belly pork (or neck) are used to impart richness to the broth.

opposite Clams, eggs, tofu... protein toppings don't have to all be meat-based.

The toppings will transform a bowl of ramen into a well-balanced dish, providing substance, flavour, texture and, of course, nutrition. The combinations are many and varied, although some ingredients appear with more frequency than others, such as pork, eggs, spring onions or scallions, sesame seeds, and chilli. Here's a guide to some of the most common ones.

PROTEIN

A protein topping is usually added in the form of meat – pork, chicken or beef – fish or seafood, tofu, and very often a marinated soft-boiled egg. Different regions favour different ways of cooking and serving these, from sticky-sweet marinated pork to curried beef and fiery chicken, and fusion flavours and techniques can also work brilliantly, such as tempura prawns atop a spicy-sour broth, or more Western pairings such as crab and lemon.

Pork A favourite meat in Japan, pork crops up again and again in many classic ramen dishes. Various cuts are used, including succulent, lean tenderloin as well as fatty belly pork, and it can be coated in a sweet-hot-savoury glaze and slow-cooked in the oven, or pan-fried with a range of strong flavourings.

Beef Flash-fried marinated steak makes a luxurious topping for a bowl of ramen, the melting texture of the tender meat providing a subtle contrast to the slippery noodles. Different cuts are slow-cooked, either as a flavouring for the broth itself or as a topping.

Poultry Chicken and duck are very popular choices for ramen, their delicate flavour allowing other subtly flavoured ingredients such as mushrooms or mild vegetables to shine. Griddled chicken is a quick option, while poaching the chicken in the stock itself is a great way to create two elements of the dish in one go.

Fish and shellfish Robust oily fish such as salmon, tuna, swordfish or mackerel are especially suitable for ramen, since their distinctive flavours marry well with other ingredients, and their relatively robust texture prevents them from disintegrating immediately, instead remaining as succulent chunks. Shellfish, and prawns/shrimp, crab, clams and scallops, as well as fish cakes (kamaboko), are suited to being lightly poached in the flavoursome broth, or cooked separately and used to top the ramen bowl, and they add some welcome texture as well as protein.

Tofu and eggs Cheap, nutritious, versatile and tasty, tofu and eggs are ideal for adding protein to vegetarian ramen, or in combination with other toppings. Eggs are usually first marinated and soft-boiled (see opposite), but are sometimes poached directly in the broth.

Marinated soft-boiled egg (ajitsuke tamago)

These delicious sweet-salt eggs are popular ramen toppings, bringing richness, texture and protein to a bowl. Once marinated, they will keep for up to 5 days in the fridge.

4 eggs
150ml/¼ pint/⅔ cup dark soy sauce
30ml/2 tbsp sake
15ml/1 tbsp sugar
15ml/1 tbsp mirin

1 Put the eggs in a small pan with cold water to cover. Place over a high heat and bring to a simmer. Once the water is simmering, set a timer and cook the eggs for 3 minutes (or a minute longer if the eggs are large). Drain immediately and put the eggs in a bowl of cold water.

2 When the eggs are just warm to the touch, drain and peel them (if they are not completely cold, peeling them is easier).

3 Put the soy sauce, sake, sugar and mirin in a small bowl. Whisk to combine and allow the sugar to dissolve.

4 Add the eggs and press them down so they are immersed in the liquid, then top with a piece of muslin or cheesecloth, making sure the edges are in the liquid so that it will soak into the fabric and keep the tops of the eggs in contact with the marinade.

5 Place in the fridge and leave to marinate for 8 hours or overnight.

6 Remove the eggs from the marinade and leave them to come to room temperature before halving them and using them to top your ramen.

Cook's tip You can keep the soy mixture after you've removed the eggs and use it as tare flavouring for the ramen broth.

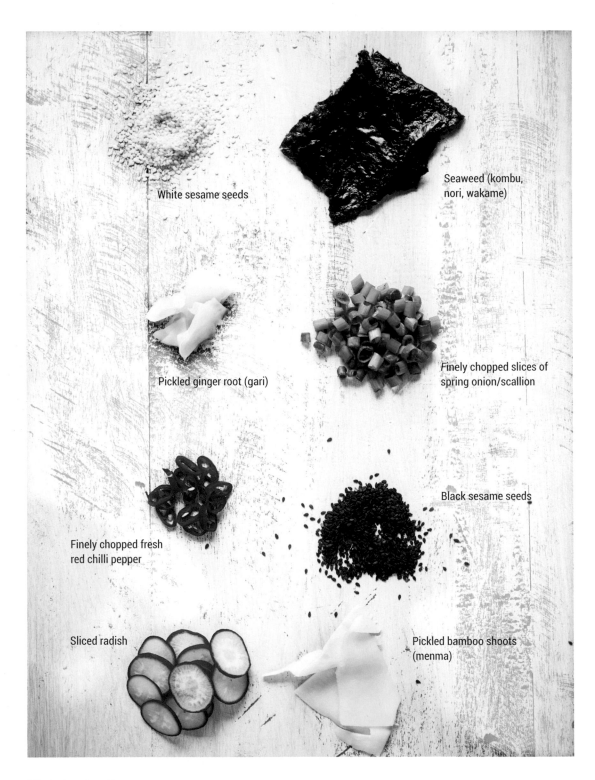

White sesame seeds

Seaweed (kombu, nori, wakame)

Pickled ginger root (gari)

Finely chopped slices of spring onion/scallion

Finely chopped fresh red chilli pepper

Black sesame seeds

Sliced radish

Pickled bamboo shoots (menma)

VEGETABLES, HERBS AND OTHER SEASONINGS

The line-up for other toppings for your ramen is vast and almost anything goes so long as it balances the flavour of the dish. Display and colour are key, as the ingredients are arranged artistically. Think about texture and taste when choosing them: fresh radish on a rich salty dish, pickled ginger to cut though the bold flavour of miso, and chilli to heat things up. These are some favourites:

Daikon or mooli Finely sliced Japanese/Chinese radish adds freshness and crunch – a winning combination that helps to balance out a rich bowl of ramen.

Pak choi/bok choy and choi sum Mild in flavour and requiring minimal cooking in the broth, these leaves are a common sight in ramen bowls and bring a little texture along with their nutritional benefits. Spinach can also be used if that's what you have to hand.

Beansprouts Crunchy and mild-flavoured, beansprouts (moyashi) are a favourite vegetable topping and can be eaten raw or very quickly cooked in the hot broth.

Sesame seeds Sprinkle over the whole seeds to add extra nuttiness to a dish, or toast and grind them in a pestle and mortar and stir into the ramen. Black sesame seeds are stronger in taste than white ones, and work especially well sprinkled on a miso ramen.

Pickled ginger The ginger used for sushi (gari) has a piquant flavour that's perfect for cutting through the richness of a pork or fish ramen.

Spring onions/scallions Finely sliced spring onions (or the Japanese allium, negi) make an appearance on most ramen, adding colour, freshness and crispness. Use the white part for a milder flavour, or the green for a more intense onion hit.

Fresh coriander/cilantro and other herbs Fragrant fresh coriander is used to top some ramen, cutting through the richness and bringing its distinctive flavour, especially to fusion dishes. Other herbs, including microherbs, can be used in the same way.

above Daikon, also known as mooli, white or winter radish, is a root vegetable that adds crispness and a peppery flavour.

below Fresh-tasting green pak choi leaves need very little cooking.

right Fresh herbs, whether mint, flat-leaf parsley, dill or others, add vibrancy and freshness.

opposite, clockwise Spring onions, fresh microherbs, fresh red chillies, kezuri-bushi (the flakes of smoked and fermented tuna fish), crunchy beansprouts, and Japanese pepper seasonings.

below Seaweed (dried wakame is pictured) adds depth of flavour and umami, as well as nutritious minerals and vitamins; it can be dried (perhaps sliced or crumbled over) or fresh for its briny taste and softer texture.

Chillies Sliced fresh red or green chillies or intense dried chilli flakes can be added to the broth as well as being sprinkled on top of a ramen to bring a bit of fire. Seeding fresh ones will reduce their potency, if you prefer less heat. Ramens are not traditionally packed with chilli.

Pickled bamboo shoots (menma) Found in Asian stores, menma is a typical ramen topping in Japan. The shoots are crunchy and fresh, which means they are ideal for topping a rich dish.

Nori, kombu and wakame A piece of seaweed is often added to ramen, either left as a slice on the side, or shredded and sprinkled all over the top. It adds a subtle aroma and saltiness as well as some added crunch, and contributes to the shio or salty element of the ramen flavouring.

Seasonings Japanese ramen can be pepped up at the table with an interesting range of seasonings. These typically include:

Shichimi togarashi – a spice blend often made from seven ingredients, usually chilli powder, dried orange peel, black and white sesame seeds, nori, hemp seeds, sansho (Sichuan) pepper, and ground ginger.

Nanami togarashi – a Japanese chilli powder that packs a real punch.

Sansho or sansyo pepper is the Japanese version of the Sichuan peppercorns from China.

Burnt garlic oil (mayu)

12 garlic cloves, peeled
50ml/2fl oz/¼ cup vegetable oil

This sticky condiment, known as mayu in Japan, is made by cooking a lot of grated or minced garlic in oil until it turns black and infuses the oil with a bitter-sweet flavour that adds depth to ramen when used sparingly. If you find it a bit much, you can combine the cooled burnt oil with a little sesame oil to round out the flavours, or maybe spice things up by adding some very finely diced fresh red chilli. Balance it all out with the addition of a pinch of sugar, if you like.

1 Grate the garlic and put it in a small pan with the oil. Place over a medium heat and cook, stirring, until the garlic starts to brown.
2 Reduce the heat to low and keep stirring and cooking until the garlic turns black – this should take about 10 minutes.

Equipment and utensils

Making ramen requires very little specialist kit and no tricksy kitchen skills, which is perhaps why the dish has become such a hit all over the world. So long as you have a chopping board, a decent knife and a pan, you can make basic ramen, although having a few other pieces of equipment will certainly enable you to produce a greater range of dishes.

Knives and chopping boards Every cook needs a good knife, and it pays to keep it sharp since it makes preparing food much quicker, easier and safer. Having a few in different sizes can be useful, ranging from a small one for fine work to a heavy one for chopping up meat and tougher vegetables. Japanese knives are especially revered, although they can be pricey. You should also have a couple of good chopping boards.

Pots and pans Given that the stock is the fundamental basis of ramen, it makes sense to make your own so that you can control every aspect. Making up a large batch and then portioning it and freezing for use at a later date is good planning, and for this you need a big pan or stock pot. If the noodles are to be cooked separately from the broth, you will also need a smaller pan, and probably at least one more, plus a frying pan or skillet, to cook the toppings. A ridged griddle pan is also useful for adding a delicious singed note to steak, chicken breasts, salmon, and some vegetables.

Utensils In addition to standard wooden spoons, it's useful to have a slotted spoon for lifting and draining noodles before dividing them up between serving bowls, as well as a ladle for transferring the broth from pan to bowl, and a colander or strainer. If you intend to make your own noodles, you'll need a rolling pin and something to drape the noodles over while they dry (or you can use the rolling pin).

Bowls and spoons Being by definition a brothy dish, ramen is always served in a deep bowl with a decent capacity so that there is plenty of space to arrange the toppings. It is also helpful to place the bowl on a plate to catch any drips, though this is not essential. Napkins, on the other hand, are… Traditionally, chopsticks are used for lifting up the noodles and toppings and bringing them to the mouth. Once the more solid elements have been eaten, the broth can then be enjoyed using a deep spoon, made from ceramic or wood, although some diners simply prefer to pick up the bowl and drink the broth. If you struggle to use chopsticks, you can of course use a fork and twist the noodles round it, spaghetti-style.

How to eat ramen like a pro

There's no pretty, or quiet, way to eat ramen. Indeed, in Japan slurping is regarded as polite since it shows the chef that you are enjoying the food. Speed is of the essence for aficionados, since the noodles continue to swell in the broth and could cause a very full bowl to overflow. The first step before you dive in, however, is to appreciate the aroma and appearance of the dish – a gustatory prelude that will whet the appetite. Next, pick up some noodles using your chopsticks and bring them to your mouth, slurping the broth as you go. Only then should you try the toppings in different combinations with the noodles, aiming, if you are a true pro, to eat the lot in 5 minutes flat. The broth can then be drunk directly from the bowl or, for the more genteel diner, spooned into the mouth. Now wipe your chin…

Pork

Char siu pork in miso ramen

Serves 4–6 | prep 30 minutes | cook 4 hours, plus overnight resting time

The key to this dish is the delicious marinade for the pork – sticky, rich and sweet, it makes a fabulous addition to the ramen bowl and contrasts really well with the saltiness of the soy sauce and the sour notes from the vinegar.

For the base
1.75 litres/3 pints/7½ cups pork stock (see page 10)
400g/14oz fresh ramen noodles

For the tare
2 garlic cloves, peeled and finely chopped
15ml/1 tbsp white miso
15ml/1 tbsp red miso
15ml/1 tbsp mirin
5ml/1 tsp demerara/raw sugar

For the char siu pork
1.2kg/2½lb belly pork
20ml/4 tsp salt
3 garlic cloves, peeled and grated
45ml/3 tbsp dark soy sauce
15ml/1 tbsp clear honey
15ml/1 tbsp demerara/raw sugar
15ml/1 tbsp rice vinegar
15ml/1 tbsp sesame oil

For the toppings
60ml/4 tbsp corn, warmed
225g/8oz/1 cup beansprouts
2 clumps of enoki mushrooms, trimmed and separated
handful of fresh micro-coriander/ cilantro leaves (or use regular sized herbs)
5ml/1 tsp black sesame seeds

1 Preheat the oven to 150°C/300°F/Gas 2. To make the char siu pork, sit the slab of belly pork in a small roasting pan, rub the skin with 15ml/3 tsp of the salt, then mix together all the remaining ingredients (reserving 5ml/1 tsp of the sesame oil for frying later) and spread the mixture all over the pork.

2 Cover the pan tightly with foil and cook the meat for 3½ hours.

3 Take out from the oven and leave to cool and rest in the pan, then remove and place the belly pork between layers of baking parchment and sit it in a dish. Put something heavy on top, to flatten it, and chill in the refrigerator overnight. Remove from the refrigerator 30 minutes before assembling the ramen.

4 When ready, slice the belly pork thickly and season with the remaining 5ml/1 tsp salt. Heat the reserved sesame oil in a small frying pan or skillet and cook the pork slices for a few minutes until golden brown on both sides. Remove and put to one side.

5 Put the stock in a large saucepan. Mix the tare ingredients together then whisk into the stock. Bring the stock to the boil, then reduce to a high simmer for 5 minutes. Taste, and adjust the seasonings as needed.

6 Put the ramen noodles in a pan of boiling water and cook for 2–3 minutes or according to packet instructions, until cooked, then remove with a slotted spoon and divide them up between the serving bowls.

7 Ladle over the hot broth, then top with belly pork slices, corn, beansprouts, mushrooms and fresh herbs. Sprinkle over a pinch of black sesame seeds and serve.

Smoky pork and bacon ramen

Serves 4 | prep 30 minutes | cook 1 hour, plus resting time

Crisp bacon ramps up the flavour and adds crunch to this tasty noodle bowl. Pork fillet is used here, which is less fatty than belly pork, but be careful not to overcook it as you want it to remain moist and tender.

For the base
1.75 litres/3 pints/7½ cups pork stock (see page 10)
400g/14oz fresh ramen noodles

For the tare
30ml/2 tbsp dark soy sauce
15ml/1 tbsp mirin
15ml/1 tbsp sake (optional)
1 cinnamon stick
2 star anise
pinch of salt

For the smoky pork
400g/14oz pork fillet/tenderloin
5cm/2in piece of fresh root ginger, peeled and grated
2 garlic cloves, peeled and grated
15ml/1 tbsp teriyaki sauce
15ml/1 tbsp tomato purée/paste
10ml/2 tsp five-spice powder
10ml/2 tsp rice vinegar
5ml/1 tsp demerara/raw sugar
5ml/1 tsp of sesame oil

For the toppings
4 rashers/strips smoked bacon
3–4 carrots, peeled and cut into fine batons
large handful of baby spinach leaves
handful of pickled bamboo shoots (menma)
15ml/1 tbsp white sesame seeds, toasted

1 Preheat the oven to 190ºC/375ºF/Gas 5. To prepare the smoky pork, mix together all the ingredients apart from the pork and sesame oil, then spread the mixture all over the meat and sit it in a small roasting pan.

2 Cover the pan tightly with foil and cook the meat for 35–40 minutes or until the pork is cooked through.

3 Take out of the oven and leave to cool and rest in the pan, then remove and place the pork in a plastic food bag or wrap it in foil or clear film/plastic wrap, and chill in the refrigerator overnight. Remove from the refrigerator 30 minutes before serving.

4 Put the stock in a large pan. Mix together the tare ingredients, add to the stock and bring to the boil. Reduce to a simmer, cook for 10 minutes, then taste and add more seasoning if necessary.

5 Preheat the grill or broiler to hot, and cook the bacon until it is crisp, then finely chop it and put it to one side. Prepare the other topping ingredients.

6 Now finish preparing the smoky pork. Heat the sesame oil in a small frying pan or skillet over a medium heat. Finely slice the pork and add it to the pan for a minute or so to heat it through.

7 Put the noodles in a pan of boiling water and cook for 2–3 minutes or according to packet instructions, until cooked, then remove with a slotted spoon and divide them up between the serving bowls.

8 Ladle over the hot broth, then top with smoky pork slices, carrot, spinach and bamboo shoots, and sprinkle with the bacon pieces and toasted sesame seeds before serving.

Sapporo-style ramen noodles in broth

Serves 4 | prep 30 minutes | cook 20 minutes

This is a rich and tangy broth from Sapporo, the capital of Hokkaido, which is Japan's most northerly island. Raw grated garlic and chilli oil are added to warm the body, while the light chicken broth nourishes the soul.

For the base
1.75 litres/3 pints/7½ cups chicken
   stock (see page 11)
400g/14oz fresh ramen noodles

For the tare
120ml/4fl oz/½ cup sake
90ml/6 tbsp miso (any colour)
30ml/2 tbsp dark soy sauce
2.5cm/1in piece of fresh root ginger,
   peeled and grated
1 garlic clove, peeled and crushed

For the toppings
115g/4oz pork belly
1 carrot
12 mangetouts/snow peas
8 baby corn
15ml/1 tbsp sesame oil
1 dried red chilli, seeded and crushed
225g/8oz/1 cup beansprouts
2 spring onions/scallions, green parts
   only, chopped
2 garlic cloves, peeled and finely
   grated
drizzle of chilli oil, to taste
pinch of salt, to taste

1 First, prepare the toppings. Cut the pork belly into 5mm/¼in slices. Peel and halve the carrot lengthways, then cut it into 3mm/⅛in thick, 5cm/2in long slices. Boil the carrot, mangetouts and corn for 3 minutes in a pan of water. Drain, rinse under cold water and set aside.

2 Heat the sesame oil in a large pan or wok and fry the pork slices and chilli. When the colour of the meat has changed, add the beansprouts. Reduce the heat to medium and add 1 litre/1¾ pints/4 cups of the chicken stock. Cook for 5 minutes.

3 Mix together the ingredients for the tare and add to the stock, then bring to the boil and cook at a steady simmer for 5 minutes. Taste and adjust the seasonings as necessary.

4 Put the noodles in a pan of boiling water and cook for 2–3 minutes or according to packet instructions, until cooked, then remove with a slotted spoon and divide them up between the serving bowls.

5 Pour the hot broth on to the noodles and heap the beansprouts and pork on top. Add the carrot, mangetouts and corn. Sprinkle with chopped spring onion and freshly grated garlic, and serve with chilli oil and a little salt if liked.

Tokyo-style ramen noodles in broth

Serves 4 | prep 30 minutes | cook 40 minutes

This legendary Tokyo ramen is just one of many regional variations featuring local specialities. Here, the broth and noodles are topped with eggs, succulent pork and pungent menma – pickled fermented bamboo shoots – among other delicious things. If liked you can use marinated soft-boiled eggs (see page 17) instead of hard-boiled.

For the base
1 litre/1¾ pints/4 cups chicken stock
 (see page 11)
400g/14oz fresh ramen noodles

For the tare
120ml/4fl oz/½ cup sake
about 60ml/4 tbsp dark soy sauce
1 garlic clove, peeled and crushed
2.5ml/½ tsp salt
2.5cm/1in piece of fresh root ginger,
 peeled and grated

For the char siu pork
500g/1lb pork shoulder, boned
30ml/2 tbsp vegetable oil
2 spring onions/scallions, chopped
2.5cm/1in piece of fresh root ginger,
 peeled and sliced
15ml/1 tbsp sake
400ml/14fl oz/1⅔ cups water
45ml/3 tbsp dark soy sauce
15ml/1 tbsp sugar

For the toppings
2 hard-boiled eggs
150g/5oz pickled bamboo shoots
 (menma), soaked for 30 minutes
 and drained
½ sheet of nori, broken into pieces
2 spring onions/scallions, sliced or
 chopped
pinch of ground white pepper
dash of sesame or chilli oil
pinch of salt, if needed

1 First, make the pork. Roll the meat up tightly to 8cm/3in diameter, then tie it with kitchen string.

2 Put the oil in a large pan or wok set over a high heat and heat it to smoking point. Add the chopped spring onions and ginger, and stir-fry for about 30 seconds, then add the meat. Turn often to brown the outside evenly.

3 Sprinkle with the sake, then add the water, shoyu and sugar. Boil, then reduce the heat to low and cover. Cook for 25–30 minutes, turning every 5 minutes. Remove from the heat.

4 Slice the pork into 12 fine slices. You can use any leftover pork for another recipe.

5 Shell and halve the eggs, then sprinkle some salt on to the yolks.

6 Put the stock in a large pan. Mix together the tare ingredients, add this to the stock and bring to the boil. Reduce to a simmer, cook for 5 minutes, then taste and add more seasoning if necessary.

7 Put the noodles in a pan of boiling water and cook for 2–3 minutes or according to packet instructions, until cooked, then remove with a slotted spoon and divide them up between the serving bowls.

8 Ladle the broth over the noodles to cover. Arrange half a boiled egg, 3 pork slices, some menma and pieces of nori on top, and sprinkle with sliced spring onions. Add a grinding or pinch of pepper and a drizzle of sesame or chilli oil. Season to taste with a little salt, if you like.

Spicy curried minced pork ramen

Serves 4 | prep 20 minutes | cook 30 minutes

This is an easy way to bring loads of flavour to the ramen as the curried pork mixture soaks into and mixes with the hot broth. Pak choi and radish add some fresh tastes and crunchy textures to the dish. Shiso is an Asian leaf with hints of basil and mint.

For the base
1.75 litres/3 pints/7½ cups chicken
    or pork stock (see pages 10–11)
400g/14oz fresh ramen noodles

For the tare
5cm/2in piece of fresh root ginger,
    peeled and roughly chopped
2 spring onions/scallions, roughly
    chopped
15ml/1 tbsp mirin
15ml/1 tbsp white miso
15ml/1 tbsp red miso
10ml/2 tsp tahini

For the spicy pork
7.5ml/1½ tsp sesame oil
1 garlic clove, peeled and finely
    chopped
1 fresh red chilli, seeded and finely
    chopped
500g/1lb minced/ground pork
pinch of salt
freshly ground black pepper
15ml/1 tbsp medium curry paste

For the toppings
2 pak choi/bok choy bulbs, trimmed
    and leaves separated
4 marinated soft-boiled eggs (see
    page 17), halved
4 radishes, trimmed and finely sliced
1 fresh green chilli, seeded and finely
    sliced
handful of purple shiso leaves or Thai
    basil (optional)
pinch of Japanese pepper (shanso)
    (optional)

1 First, prepare the spicy pork. Heat the sesame oil in a large frying pan or skillet over a medium-high heat, then add the garlic and chilli and cook for 1 minute. Add the pork, season with salt and pepper, and stir around the pan to break the meat up.

2 Stir in the curry paste until well combined, then cook the mixture for about 15 minutes or until the pork is no longer pink. Reduce the heat to very low and simmer, stirring occasionally, until required.

3 Add all the ingredients for the tare to a food processor and blitz until smooth. Transfer the mixture to a small frying pan and cook on a low simmer for a few minutes.

4 Put the stock in a large pan. Give the simmered tare ingredients a stir, add to the stock and bring to the boil. Reduce to a simmer, cook for 5 minutes, then taste and add more seasoning if necessary.

5 Put the pak choi in a pan of boiling salted water and cook for 2–3 minutes. Remove with a slotted spoon and put to one side.

6 Add the noodles to the water and cook for 2–3 minutes or according to packet instructions, until soft, then remove with a slotted spoon and transfer to the serving bowls.

7 Ladle over hot stock, then spoon in the pork mince and top with the pak choi, eggs, radish, chilli and shiso if using. Sprinkle with Japanese pepper if you like, and serve.

Thai-style pork and peanut ramen

Serves 4 | prep 30 minutes | cook 1 hour

This is a fusion of cuisines and is full of gutsy flavours. Chicken stock is used as the broth but you can switch to a heavier pork one if you prefer. The pork is tender and lean and tastes wonderful paired with fresh beansprouts and a zing of lime.

For the base
1.75 litres/3 pints/7½ cups chicken
   or pork stock (see pages 10–11)
400g/14oz fresh ramen noodles

For the tare
15–30ml/1–2 tbsp red miso
15ml/1 tbsp dark soy sauce
15ml/1 tbsp mirin
pinch of salt

For the Thai pork
400g/14oz pork fillet/tenderloin
30ml/2 tbsp dark soy sauce
15ml/1 tbsp smooth peanut butter
10ml/2 tsp Thai red curry paste
10ml/2 tsp fish sauce
juice of 1 lime
pinch of salt
freshly ground black pepper
drizzle of sesame oil

For the toppings
large handful of fresh beansprouts
large handful of fresh coriander/
   cilantro leaves
2–3 spring onions/scallions, green
   parts only, finely chopped
1 fresh red chilli, seeded and finely
   sliced
handful of roasted peanuts, chopped
2 limes, halved

1 Preheat the oven to 190°C/375°F/Gas 5.

2 To prepare the Thai pork, mix all the ingredients together except the sesame oil. Smother the mixture all over the pork to cover, then heat the sesame oil in a frying pan, add the pork and sear it on both sides until golden.

3 Remove the pork and transfer it to a roasting pan, cover it tightly with foil and put it in the oven for about 35–40 minutes or until the pork is cooked through. Remove and put to one side to rest before slicing thinly.

4 Put the stock in a large pan. Mix together the tare ingredients, add to the stock and bring to the boil. Reduce to a simmer, cook for 5 minutes, then taste and add more seasoning if necessary.

5 Put the noodles in a pan of boiling water and cook for 2–3 minutes or according to packet instructions, until cooked, then remove with a slotted spoon and divide them up between the serving bowls.

6 Ladle over hot stock, then top with the sliced pork, beansprouts and fresh coriander, and scatter over the chopped spring onions, chilli and peanuts. Serve with a lime half in each bowl.

COOK'S TIP: You can cook the pork the day before, then leave it to cool, wrap it in clear film/plastic wrap and keep it in the refrigerator. When you are ready to eat the dish, slice the pork and reheat it in a little hot sesame oil in a frying pan or skillet.

Pork and mushroom ramen

serves 4 | prep 30 minutes | cook 2 hours

This substantial ramen-esque noodle dish makes good use of the multitude of cultivated mushrooms that are grown in abundance in Asia, using them both to make a flavoursome broth and as a crowning glory on top of the noodles, alongside slices of roast pork, a soft-boiled egg, chilli oil and shreds of dried seaweed.

For the base
1 litre/1¾ pints/4 cups of boiling water
30g/1¼oz/½ cup mixed dried mushrooms
400g/14oz fresh ramen noodles

For the tare
30ml/2 tbsp sake or rice vinegar
15ml/1 tbsp Chinese five-spice powder
10ml/2 tsp chilli powder
10ml/2 tsp palm sugar
5cm/2in piece of fresh root ginger, peeled and sliced
1 garlic clove, peeled
pinch of ground white pepper

For the pork
700g/1½lb pork shoulder
30ml/2 tbsp vegetable oil
15ml/1 tbsp soy sauce
1 garlic clove, peeled and crushed

For the toppings
400g/14oz shimeji, enoki and nameko mushrooms
2 eryngii and matsutake mushrooms, sliced lengthways
4–6 soft-boiled eggs
1 sheet of nori, snipped into ribbons
2 spring onions/scallions, shredded lengthways
1 garlic clove, peeled and sliced
1 fresh red chilli, chopped
ground white pepper

1 Preheat the oven to 230°C/450°F/Gas 8. To prepare the pork, first place the joint in a roasting pan. In a small bowl, mix together the oil, soy sauce and the crushed garlic, then coat the pork with the mixture. Roast for 30 minutes, then turn the oven down to 180°C/350°F/Gas 4 for a further hour. Let the pork stand for 20 minutes, then slice.

2 Meanwhile, make the base stock by putting the measured boiling water and the dried mushrooms in a large jug or pitcher and leaving to stand for 10 minutes.

3 In a large pan, combine the rehydrated mushrooms and their soaking liquid, the sake, Chinese five-spice, chilli powder, palm sugar, ginger, the whole garlic clove, and white pepper. Add the fresh mushrooms listed in the toppings. Bring to the boil, then simmer for 10 minutes.

4 Meanwhile, put the noodles in a pan of boiling water and cook for 2–3 minutes or according to packet instructions, until cooked, then remove with a slotted spoon and divide them up between the serving bowls.

5 Ladle over the broth with the mushrooms, then top with halved boiled eggs, the shredded nori, spring onion shreds, sliced garlic and chopped chilli. Season with more pepper if liked, and serve.

Tonkotsu ramen with braised pork

Serves 4–6 | prep 30 minutes | cook 4 hours, plus resting time

This speciality ramen dish from the Kyushu island of the Fukuoka Prefecture in Japan is made using pork bone broth – 'tonkotsu' means 'pork bones' – and is topped with braised pork belly. It is one of the most-loved and well-known ramen dishes, and often goes by the name hakata ramen.

For the base
1.75 litres/3 pints/7½ cups pork
  stock (see page 10)
400g/14oz fresh ramen noodles

For the tare
30ml/2 tbsp dark soy sauce
15ml/1 tbsp rice vinegar
15ml/1 tbsp mirin
15ml/1 tbsp sake (optional)

For the braised pork
600g/1lb 6oz piece of tightly rolled
  belly pork (you can ask your
  butcher to do this)
500ml/17fl oz/generous 2 cups water
200ml/7fl oz/scant 1 cup dark soy
  sauce
100ml/3½fl oz/scant ½ cup mirin
15ml/1 tbsp demerara/raw sugar
2–3 spring onions/scallions, roughly
  chopped
5cm/2in piece of fresh root ginger,
  peeled and roughly chopped

For the toppings
200g/7oz shiitake mushrooms, large
  ones halved
4–6 marinated soft-boiled eggs (see
  page 17), halved
2–3 spring onions/scallions, green
  parts only, finely chopped
pinch of Japanese chilli (nanami
  togarashi) or dried chilli flakes
pinch of black sesame seeds
handful of purple shiso leaves
  (optional)

1 Preheat the oven to 150ºC/300ºF/Gas 2. To prepare the pork, put it in a large lidded ovenproof pan (or you can use a roasting pan and cover it tightly with foil). Add the measured water and all the other ingredients and cook for 3½ hours, taking a look at it occasionally and topping up with a little water if necessary.

2 Remove the pan from the oven and leave it to cool (see Cook's Tip) in the cooking liquid. Once cold, lift the meat out of the braising cooking liquid and set both aside.

3 Put the base stock in a large pan and bring it to the boil, then stir in all the tare ingredients and a few spoonfuls of the braised pork cooking liquid. Reduce to a simmer and cook for 10–15 minutes for the flavours to mingle, then taste and season with salt if necessary or adjust with more soy sauce or mirin.

4 Put the remaining braised pork cooking liquid in a shallow frying pan or skillet. Finely slice the pork and add it to the pan. Simmer for a few minutes to reheat the pork.

5 Put the noodles in a pan of boiling water and cook for 2–3 minutes or according to packet instructions, until cooked, then remove with a slotted spoon and divide them up between the serving bowls.

6 Ladle over the hot broth, then top with the pork slices, shiitake mushrooms, marinated egg halves, chopped spring onions, a pinch of the chilli pepper and a sprinkle of black sesame seeds, and finishing with a few shiso leaves, if using. Serve.

COOK'S TIP: Get ahead and cook the belly pork the day before. Leave it to cool completely in its cooking liquid, then remove and put it in a plastic food bag in the refrigerator until required. Store the cooking liquid separately as you will need it. Remove the pork from the refrigerator 30 minutes before serving. This get-ahead method will also enable you to slice the meat more easily and finely.

Beef

Shoyu beef and Chinese leaf ramen

Serves 4 | prep 20 minutes | cook 30 minutes

This pure-tasting ramen dish uses a light stock base made from chicken rather than pork or beef, since this allows the flavour of the finely sliced beef and the delicate taste of the Chinese leaf to shine through. Seaweed adds to the umami notes, as well as contributing briny salinity.

For the base
1.75 litres/3 pints/7½ cups chicken stock (see page 11)
400g/14oz fresh ramen noodles

For the tare
30ml/2 tbsp tamari soy sauce
30ml/2 tbsp dark soy sauce
15ml/1 tbsp mirin
pinch of salt

For the beef
400g/14oz rump steak
15ml/1 tbsp light soy sauce
10ml/2 tsp mirin
pinch of salt and ground black pepper
15ml/1 tbsp of sunflower oil, or as needed to fry

For the toppings
30ml/2 tbsp sesame oil
2 garlic cloves, peeled and grated
about ½ head of Chinese leaves/cabbage, shredded
2–3 spring onions/scallions, green tops only, finely sliced
1 sheet of nori seaweed, broken into pieces
pinch of Japanese chilli powder (nanami togarashi) or dried chilli flakes
pinch of black sesame seeds

1 First, prepare the beef. Put the steak on a plate, mix together the soy sauce, mirin, salt and pepper, and pour it over the steak. Turn to coat.

2 Heat the sunflower oil in a frying pan or skillet over a medium-high heat, then add the steak and cook for about 4 minutes each side, depending on the thickness and your preference. Remove to a plate and leave to rest before slicing finely.

3 For the toppings, heat the sesame oil in a small frying pan or skillet, then add the garlic and cook until sizzling and starting to darken. Remove the garlicky oil from the heat and put aside.

4 Put the stock in a large pan. Mix together the tare ingredients, add to the stock and bring to the boil. Reduce to a simmer, cook for 5 minutes, then taste and add more seasoning if necessary.

5 Meanwhile, put the noodles in a pan of boiling water and cook for 2–3 minutes or according to packet instructions, until cooked, then remove with a slotted spoon and divide them up between the serving bowls.

6 Ladle over the hot broth, then top with slices of beef, shredded Chinese leaves, sliced spring onion, and a piece or two of nori seaweed. Drizzle over some of the garlic oil, then sprinkle with a little Japanese chilli or chilli flakes and black sesame seeds, then serve.

Cold beef broth with buckwheat ramen

Serves 4 | prep 20 minutes, plus 30 minutes soaking | cook 1 hour 20 minutes, plus chilling

The refreshing properties of this chilled broth, naengmyeon, make it a popular summer dish in Korea. The buckwheat noodles float in a traditional broth, which is flavoured with tare ingredients that are added at the end, rather than during the cooking, as with most Japanese ramens.

For the beef base
200g/7oz beef shank
1.75 litres/3 pints/7½ cups water, plus extra for soaking
2 leeks, roughly chopped
1 onion, peeled and roughly chopped
10g/½oz fresh root ginger, peeled and roughly chopped
6 garlic cloves, peeled and chopped
250g/9oz dried buckwheat noodles or dried ramen noodles

For the tare
20ml/4 tsp rice vinegar, to taste
10ml/2 tsp ready-made English/hot mustard, to taste
5ml/1 tsp sugar, or to taste
5ml/1 tsp salt, or to taste

For the pickled radish
½ white radish (daikon), peeled
30ml/2 tbsp rice vinegar
30ml/2 tbsp sugar
2.5ml/½ tsp salt

For the toppings
1 cucumber
2 Asian pears
a little lemon juice
8 ice cubes
2 hard-boiled eggs, halved

1 Place the beef in a bowl of cold water, leave it to soak for 30 minutes, then drain. Pour the measured water into a pan and bring to the boil. Add the beef and reduce the heat. Simmer for 1 hour, skimming the fat from the surface.

2 Add the leek, onion, ginger and garlic, and cook for another 20 minutes. Remove the meat and when cool enough to handle, cut into thin slices.

3 Strain the cooking broth into a jug or pitcher. Cool, then chill in the refrigerator.

4 Meanwhile, prepare the pickled radish. Cut the daikon into thin strips, then put them in a bowl and add the rice vinegar and sugar and a little salt. Coat the daikon and leave it to chill.

5 For the toppings, seed the cucumber and cut it into thin strips. Peel and core the pears and cut it into strips (sprinkle with lemon juice to prevent discolouring).

6 Put the noodles in a pan of boiling water and cook for 5 minutes, or as on the packet instructions. Drain and rinse two or three times in cold water until the water runs clear. Chill in the refrigerator.

7 Pour the chilled broth into individual bowls, adding a couple of ice cubes to each. Add a portion of noodles and divide the sliced beef, cucumber, pear and pickled radish between them. Top each with half an egg.

8 Place the tare seasonings in separate small dishes and serve with the bowls of broth at the table. The individual diner stirs the seasonings into their broth to suit their taste: start with 5ml/1 tsp of vinegar and 2.5ml/½ tsp mustard, with a pinch of sugar and also of salt.

Teriyaki beef ramen with pickled vegetables

Serves 4 | prep 20 minutes, plus 20 minutes marinating | cook 30 minutes

For the base
1.75 litres/3 pints/7½ cups chicken or
    pork stock (see pages 10–11)
400g/14oz fresh ramen noodles

For the tare
15ml/1 tbsp red miso
15ml/1 tbsp white miso
15ml/1 tbsp light soy sauce
15ml/1 tbsp mirin
5cm/2in piece of fresh root ginger,
    peeled and finely grated

For the teriyaki beef
400g/14oz rump steak
45ml/3 tbsp mirin
30ml/2 tbsp dark soy sauce
30ml/2 tbsp sake
15ml/1 tbsp caster/superfine sugar
10ml/2 tsp clear honey
5cm/2in piece of fresh root ginger,
    peeled and grated
1 garlic clove, peeled and grated
15ml/1 tbsp sesame oil

For the pickled vegetables
2–3 carrots, peeled and finely sliced
large handful of radishes, trimmed and
    finely sliced
½ cucumber, finely sliced
45ml/3 tbsp mirin
5ml/1 tsp caster/superfine sugar
pinch of salt

For the toppings
1 small head of broccoli, broken into
    small florets
15–30ml/1–2 tbsp pickled ginger
    (gari)
15ml/1 tbsp white sesame seeds,
    toasted
2 limes, halved

The piquant radish and carrot toppings in this dish balance the richness of the broth perfectly, while the pickled ginger and lime also add lightness to the savoury umami miso-based ramen.

1 To make the teriyaki beef, put the steak in a shallow dish. Mix all its flavouring ingredients together except the sesame oil, to make a sauce, pour this over the meat, turn to coat and leave to marinate for 20 minutes.

2 When you are ready to cook, heat the sesame oil in a frying pan or skillet, add the steak and cook for about 4 minutes on each side, depending on thickness and personal preference. Remove to a plate and put to one side to rest.

3 To make the pickled vegetables, put the sliced carrots, radishes and cucumber in a small bowl. Mix the mirin and sugar together then add a pinch of salt. Pour this mixture over the vegetables and stir well so they all get coated. Set aside.

4 Put the stock in a large pan. Mix together the tare ingredients, add to the stock and bring to the boil. Reduce to a simmer, cook for 5 minutes, then taste and add more seasoning if necessary.

5 Cook the broccoli in a pan of boiling water for about 4–5 minutes, until just tender, then remove with a slotted spoon and put to one side.

6 Put the noodles in a pan of boiling water and cook for 2–3 minutes or according to packet instructions, until cooked, then remove with a slotted spoon and divide them up between the serving bowls. Pour over the broth.

7 Finely slice the steak and add to the bowls, then top with the broccoli, pickled ginger and pickled vegetables. Sprinkle over toasted sesame seeds and top with lime halves to serve.

COOK'S TIP: If you have any leftover pickled vegetables, they can be kept in the refrigerator and enjoyed the next day.

Beef ramen with oyster mushrooms

Serves 2 | prep 20 minutes | cook 40 minutes

Colloquially known as 'marketplace noodles', this has long been enjoyed as a quick and simple lunch in many parts of Asia. Here, the cooking liquor from the beef is used as the broth, rather than a separate stock, which makes the dish even easier to whip up. Just double the quantities to serve 4.

For the beef base
500ml/17fl oz/generous 2 cups water
75g/3oz beef, such as rump steak
225g/8oz fresh ramen noodles

For the tare
30ml/2 tbsp light soy sauce

For the toppings
2 eggs, beaten
45ml/3 tbsp vegetable oil
4 oyster mushrooms
75g/3oz courgette/zucchini
5ml/1 tsp sesame oil, for drizzling
1 spring onion/scallion, finely
    chopped
1 dried red chilli, finely sliced
2 garlic cloves, peeled and crushed
5ml/1 tsp white sesame seeds,
    toasted
salt and ground white pepper, to taste

1 Pour the water for the base into a pan and bring it to the boil. Add the beef steak and cook for about 20 minutes, until tender. Remove the meat and set to one side; when cool enough, slice it into thin strips.

2 Strain the cooking liquid through a sieve or strainer into a jug or bowl, add the light soy sauce and then set to one side.

3 Season the beaten eggs with a pinch of salt. Coat a frying pan or skillet with 15ml/1 tbsp of the vegetable oil and put over a medium heat. Add the egg, swirling the pan to spread it evenly, and make a thin omelette. Cook until set and lightly browned on each side.

4 Slide the omelette from the pan on to a board and roll it up, then slice it thinly and shake out the slices into thin strips.

5 Cut the oyster mushrooms and courgette into thin strips. Sprinkle both with a little salt. Pat dry with kitchen paper after 5 minutes.

6 Heat the remaining vegetable oil in a wok over a medium heat. Quickly stir-fry the mushrooms and drizzle with sesame oil before setting them aside. Add and lightly fry the courgette until softened, then remove. Finally, stir-fry the beef strips until lightly browned, and set aside.

7 Bring a pan of water to the boil. Add the noodles and bring back to the boil. Cook for 2–3 minutes, or according to the packet instructions, until just tender. Drain the noodles and rinse in cold water. Leave to drain again, then divide between serving bowls.

8 Quickly reheat the reserved beef stock. Cover with the mushrooms, courgette and strips of beef. Top with the spring onion, chilli and garlic, then pour over the beef stock to part-fill the bowls. Top with omelette strips and finally, sprinkle with sesame seeds, and a grinding of white pepper if you like.

Miso steak and tomato ramen

Serves 4 | prep 20 minutes, plus marinating time | cook 30 minutes

Tomatoes are perhaps not as authentic as some of the classic toppings for ramen but do work well, since they gently 'poach' in the hot stock, and add a fabulous sweetness and softness that contrasts with the crunch of the raw sugar snaps.

For the base
1.75 litres/3 pints/7½ cups chicken
    or pork stock (see pages 10–11)
400g/14oz fresh ramen noodles

For the tare
2 garlic cloves, peeled and grated
5cm/2in piece of fresh root ginger,
    peeled and grated
15ml/1 tbsp white miso
15ml/1 tbsp red miso
15ml/1 tbsp mirin
10ml/2 tsp tahini
5ml/1 tsp chilli paste

For the miso steak
400g/14oz rump steak
15ml/1 tbsp white miso
15ml/1 tbsp mirin

For the toppings
handful of cherry tomatoes, halved
large handful of sugar snap peas,
    sliced on the diagonal
30ml/2 tbsp pickled bamboo shoots
    (menma)
1 sheet of nori, torn into four pieces
10ml/2 tsp black sesame seeds

1 First, prepare the steak. Mix together the miso and mirin in a shallow bowl, then add the steak and turn to coat it in the marinade. Cover and leave to marinate for 15 minutes.

2 When you are ready to cook, put a frying pan or skillet over a high heat until it is hot, then add the steak and fry it for about 4 minutes on each side, until it is just cooked (the time will depend on the thickness of the steak and personal preference). Remove to a plate and set aside to rest.

3 Put the stock in a large pan and place over a medium heat while you prepare the tare.

4 To prepare the tare, heat a small pan over a high heat. Once hot, put the garlic and ginger in the pan and cook, stirring, for a few seconds. Reduce the heat to medium and add the remaining tare ingredients. Simmer, stirring continually, for 2–3 minutes.

5 Whisk the tare into the stock and bring to the boil, then reduce the heat and simmer for 5 minutes until piping hot. Taste and adjust the seasonings as needed.

6 Meanwhile, put the noodles in a pan of boiling water and cook for 2–3 minutes or according to packet instructions, until cooked, then remove with a slotted spoon and divide them up between the serving bowls.

7 Ladle the hot broth over the noodles. Slice the steak and lay it on the noodles, then top with the tomatoes, sugar snaps and pickled bamboo shoots. Sit a piece of nori at the side of each bowl and sprinkle over sesame seeds to serve.

Vietnamese-style beef ramen

Serves 6 | prep 30 minutes | cook 4 hours 30 minutes

The iconic Vietnamese noodle broth, pho, is traditionally made with rice noodles, but it works well using ramen noodles. This version is intensely beefy, being made with two cuts of meat: oxtail, slow-cooked with aromatics to produce a flavoured broth; and sirloin, sliced into wafer-thin strips and cooked only when the hot broth is poured over.

For the pho base

1.5kg/3lb 5oz oxtail, trimmed of fat
   and cut into thick pieces
2 large onions, peeled and quartered
2 carrots, peeled and cut into chunks
7.5cm/3in piece of fresh root ginger,
   peeled and chopped
6 cloves
2 cinnamon sticks
6 star anise
5ml/1 tsp black peppercorns
400g/14oz fresh ramen noodles

For the tare

30ml/2 tbsp soy sauce
45–60ml/3–4 tbsp nuoc mam
pinch of salt

For the toppings

250g/9oz beef sirloin
1 onion, peeled and finely sliced
6–8 spring onions/scallions, cut into
   long pieces
2–3 fresh red Thai chillies, seeded
   and finely sliced
115g/4oz/½ cup beansprouts
1 large bunch each of fresh coriander/
   cilantro and mint, stalks removed
   and leaves chopped
2 limes, quartered
hoisin sauce, nuoc mam or nuoc
   cham, to serve

1 To make the pho base, put the oxtail into a large, deep pan and cover with water. Bring to the boil and blanch the meat for 10–15 minutes. Drain the meat, rinsing off any scum, and clean the pan.

2 Put the blanched oxtail back into the pan with the other pho base ingredients (except the noodles), and add the soy sauce from the tare. Cover with about 3 litres/5¼ pints/12 cups water, bring it to the boil, reduce the heat and simmer, covered, for 2–3 hours.

3 Remove the lid and simmer for another hour, until the stock has reduced to about 2 litres/3½ pints/8 cups. Skim off any fat and then strain the stock into another pan. Discard the oxtail, which has played its part by flavouring the broth.

4 Cut the beef sirloin against the grain into very thin pieces. Bring the stock to the boil once more, stir in the nuoc mam from the tare, season to taste with salt, then reduce the heat and leave the stock simmering gently until ready to use.

5 Put the noodles in a pan of boiling water and cook for 2–3 minutes or according to packet instructions, until cooked, then remove with a slotted spoon and divide between serving bowls.

6 Top each bowl with the slices of beef, onion, spring onion and chilli. Ladle in piping-hot broth, top with the beansprouts and fresh herbs, and serve with lime wedges to squeeze over. Pass around the hoisin sauce, nuoc mam or nuoc cham for those who like a little sweetening, fish flavouring, or extra fire.

COOK'S TIPS:
• The key to pho is this tasty, light broth flavoured with ginger, cinnamon, cloves and star anise, so it is worth cooking it slowly and leaving it to stand overnight to allow the flavours to develop fully.
• The fine slices of rare, tender beef cook gently under the steaming stock that is spooned over the top.

Curried beef ramen

Serves 4 | prep 20 minutes | cook 25 minutes

Chunky pieces of curried beef add texture and intense flavour to this Indian-influenced ramen dish, enhanced with the addition of curry paste to the tare. Sliced fresh chilli dials up the heat, but leave it out if you prefer things less fiery.

For the base
1.75 litres/3 pints/7½ cups chicken stock (see page 11)
400g/14oz fresh ramen noodles

For the tare
15–30ml/1–2 tbsp medium curry paste
15ml/1 tbsp light soy sauce
15ml/1 tbsp mirin
15ml/1 tbsp sake
15ml/1 tbsp rice vinegar
pinch of salt

For the curried beef
500g/1lb beef skirt, cut into chunky cubes
10–20ml/2–4 tsp medium curry paste
15ml/1 tbsp sesame oil
1 fresh red chilli, seeded and finely chopped
5cm/2in piece of fresh root ginger, peeled and grated
pinch of ground turmeric
salt and ground black pepper

For the toppings
large handful of baby spinach leaves
1 fresh red chilli, finely chopped
2–3 spring onions/scallions, green parts only, finely sliced
handful of micro or regular coriander/cilantro leaves

1 First, season the beef with salt and pepper, then toss it in the curry paste. Heat the oil in a large frying pan over a medium-high heat, then add the beef and cook until golden on all sides – you may need to do this in batches depending on the size of your pan.

2 Add the chilli and ginger and cook for a minute more, then stir in the turmeric, turning the meat to coat, and cook for a couple more minutes. Remove the pan from the heat and put to one side.

3 Put the stock in a large pan. Mix together the tare ingredients, add to the stock and bring to the boil. Reduce to a simmer, cook for 5 minutes, then taste and add more seasoning if necessary.

4 Put the noodles in a pan of boiling water and cook for 2–3 minutes or according to packet instructions, until cooked, then remove with a slotted spoon and divide them up between the serving bowls.

5 Ladle over the piping-hot broth, add the curried beef, then top with spinach leaves, chilli, spring onion and coriander leaves to serve.

Poultry

Griddled chicken and mushroom ramen

Serves 4 | prep 20 minutes | cook 40 minutes

The chicken that tops this substantial ramen dish is coated with a barbecue sauce then cooked on a hot griddle to add a delectable charred flavour. It would also be great grilled on a barbecue to add some smokiness to the sweetness.

For the base
1.75 litres/3 pints/7½ cups pork
    stock (see page 10)
400g/14oz fresh ramen noodles

For the tare
30ml/2 tbsp dark soy sauce
15ml/1 tbsp black rice vinegar
15ml/1 tbsp clear honey
15ml/1 tbsp tomato purée/paste
pinch of dried chilli flakes
drizzle of sesame oil

For the griddled chicken
4 chicken breast portions, skin on
15ml/1 tbsp sesame oil
15ml/1 tbsp black rice vinegar
10ml/2 tsp clear honey
10ml/2 tsp tomato purée/paste
pinch of salt and ground black pepper

For the toppings
300g/10½ oz/scant 4 cups button/
    white mushrooms
drizzle of light soy sauce
drizzle of sesame oil
300g/10½ oz/scant 2 cups corn,
    warmed
pinch of Japanese chilli (nanami
    togarashi)
pinch of black sesame seeds
    (optional)
fresh coriander/cilantro leaves, to
    garnish

1 Preheat the oven to 200ºC/400ºF/Gas 6.

2 First, prepare the chicken. Mix together the sesame oil, vinegar, honey, tomato paste, and salt and pepper in a bowl, then add the chicken portions and turn to coat thoroughly.

3 Heat a griddle pan until it is really hot, then add the chicken breasts, two at a time, and cook for about 5 minutes, until char lines appear. Turn and cook the other side for a further 5 minutes.

4 Transfer the chicken to a roasting pan and place in the oven to finish off cooking for 10–15 minutes. Remove from the oven and leave to rest in the pan for 5 minutes, then slice the chicken on the diagonal and put to one side.

5 Put the stock in a large pan. Mix together the tare ingredients, add to the stock and bring to the boil. Reduce to a simmer, cook for about 10 minutes, then taste and add more seasoning if necessary.

6 For the toppings, toss the mushrooms with a little soy sauce in a bowl. Heat the sesame oil in a frying pan or skillet, then add the mushrooms and cook for 3–4 minutes.

7 Put the noodles in a pan of boiling water and cook for 2–3 minutes or according to packet instructions, until cooked, then remove with a slotted spoon and divide them up between the serving bowls.

8 Add the corn kernels to the hot broth to heat through, then remove with a slotted spoon and spoon them over the noodles. Ladle over the hot stock, then arrange the chicken slices on top. Finish with the mushrooms, add a pinch of Japanese pepper and black sesame seeds if you like, and garnish with fresh herb leaves.

Spicy seasoned chicken and vegetable ramen

Serves 4 | prep 30 minutes | cook 45 minutes

For the base
½ chicken, about 500g/1lb
2 leeks
4 garlic cloves, peeled
40g/1½oz fresh root ginger, peeled
approx 1.75 litres/3 pints/7½ cups
    water
400g/14oz fresh ramen noodles

For the tare
drizzle of light soy sauce
salt and ground white pepper, to taste

For the chicken seasoning
30ml/2 tbsp sesame oil
30ml/2 tbsp sesame seeds
10ml/2 tsp dark soy sauce
2 spring onions/scallions, finely
    chopped
2 garlic cloves, peeled and crushed
a pinch of salt and ground white
    pepper

For the toppings
8 dried shiitake mushrooms
30ml/2 tbsp vegetable oil
115g/4oz carrot, peeled and cut into
    strips
1 courgette/zucchini, cut into strips
1 onion, finely chopped
10ml/2 tsp sesame oil
½ dried chilli, finely chopped
salt and ground white pepper, to taste

For the sauce
30ml/2 tbsp light soy sauce
15ml/1 tbsp sesame oil
10ml/2 tsp Korean chilli powder
10ml/2 tsp sesame seeds
2 spring onions/scallions, finely
    chopped
2 garlic cloves, peeled and crushed

Here, the noodles are cooked in a hot home-made chicken broth and topped with vegetable strips, seasoned chicken shreds, and a dash of spicy sauce, to make a really satisfying dish.

1 First, make the base stock. Portion the chicken into large pieces and place in a large pan. Add the leeks, garlic and ginger, and enough of the water to cover. Bring to the boil over a medium heat and boil for about 35 minutes, or until the chicken is tender. Remove the chicken and strain the liquid into a jug or pitcher.

2 Meanwhile, as the chicken is cooking, put the dried shiitake mushrooms in a bowl of warm water for about 30 minutes until softened.

3 When cooked, skin and bone the chicken and tear the meat into thin strips. Mix the chicken seasoning ingredients in a bowl with salt and pepper. Add the chicken strips, coat with the seasoning and set aside.

4 Now prepare the toppings. Drain the shiitake mushrooms and slice them, discarding the stems. Heat the vegetable oil in a frying pan or skillet and lightly stir-fry the mushrooms, carrot strips, courgette strips, and onion slices. Drizzle over the sesame oil, season with salt and pepper, and set aside.

5 Combine all the sauce ingredients in a dish, adding a little water if required.

6 Bring the chicken stock to the boil in a large pan, then add the tare soy sauce and seasoning. Add the noodles and cook for 2–3 minutes or according to packet instructions, until cooked, then remove with a slotted spoon and divide them up between the serving bowls.

7 Ladle the hot broth over the noodles. Top with the chicken strips and all the topping vegetables including a little dried chilli. Stir a spoonful of the sauce into each bowl just before eating.

Fried chilli chicken ramen

Serves 4 | prep 20 minutes | cook 30 minutes

This is a riot of flavours, rich and filling. The incredibly moreish crispy chicken is tossed in cornflour before being fried, resulting in a golden crunchy outer coating that contrasts beautifully with the silky noodles. It is all topped with a burnt garlic oil, which is often used on ramen dishes and brings a slight bitterness to the party.

For the base
1.75 litres/3 pints/7½ cups chicken stock (see page 11)
400g/14oz fresh ramen noodles

For the tare
30ml/2 tbsp dark soy sauce
15ml/1 tbsp black rice vinegar
15ml/1 tbsp mirin
5ml/1 tsp sambal chilli sauce
salt and ground black pepper, to taste

For the chilli chicken
2–3 chicken breast portions, cut into chunky pieces
30–45ml/2–3 tbsp sesame oil
1 garlic clove, peeled and finely chopped
15ml/1 tbsp black rice vinegar
10ml/2 tsp clear honey
5ml/1 tsp sambal chilli sauce
salt and ground pepper
about 30ml/2 tbsp cornflour/cornstarch

For the toppings
20ml/4 tsp burnt garlic oil, see page 21 (optional)
3–4 radishes, trimmed and finely sliced
2 fresh green chillies, finely sliced
2–3 spring onions/scallions, green parts only, finely sliced

1 First, prepare the chicken. Mix together in a bowl 15ml/1 tbsp of the sesame oil with the garlic, vinegar, honey, sambal, and salt and pepper. Add the chicken pieces and toss to coat.

2 While the chicken is marinating, put the stock in a large pan. Mix together the ingredients for the tare and whisk it into the stock, bring to the boil, then reduce to a simmer and cook for 5–10 minutes. Taste and adjust the seasoning if necessary.

3 Tip the cornflour on to a plate. Heat the remaining sesame oil in a wok or large frying pan until hot. Working with a few chunks at a time, toss the chicken pieces in flour and add to the oil. Cook until the chicken is cooked through and crispy and golden all over, then transfer to a plate and repeat with the rest of the chicken, adding more oil if necessary. Put to one side.

4 Put the noodles in a pan of boiling water and cook for 2–3 minutes or according to packet instructions, until cooked, then remove with a slotted spoon and divide them up between the serving bowls.

5 Ladle over the hot broth and top with crispy chicken pieces. Spoon over the garlic oil, if using, then top with radishes, chillies and spring onions to serve.

Fiery chicken ramen-style with crispy noodles

Serves 4 | prep 30 minutes | cook 30–40 minutes

Nowadays a signature dish of the city of Chiang Mai in Thailand, this delicious ramen-style soup combines spice, saltiness and sourness in a creamy coconut-milk broth, with crispy-fried noodles as well as the wet noodles for textural contrast.

For the base
600ml/1 pint/2½ cups chicken stock
   (see page 11)
400g/14oz fresh ramen noodles

For the tare
60ml/4 tbsp Thai fish sauce
15ml/1 tbsp dark soy sauce
juice of ½–1 lime, to taste
salt and ground black pepper, to taste

For the spicy chicken
500g/1lb chicken thighs, boned and
   cut into bitesize chunks
600ml/1 pint/2½ cups coconut milk
30ml/2 tbsp Thai red curry paste
5ml/1 tsp ground turmeric

For the toppings
4 dried noodle nests
vegetable oil, for deep-frying
3 spring onions/scallions, sliced
4 fresh red chillies, seeded and sliced
   into thin strips
4 shallots, sliced
60ml/4 tbsp sliced pickled mustard
   leaves, rinsed
2 garlic cloves, peeled, sliced and
   fried
fresh coriander/cilantro leaves,
   chopped, to garnish

1 First, prepare the chicken. Pour about one-third of the coconut milk into a large, heavy pan or wok. Bring to the boil over a medium heat, stirring frequently with a wooden spoon until the milk separates.

2 Add the curry paste and ground turmeric, stir to mix completely and cook for 2–3 minutes or until the mixture is fragrant. Add the chunks of chicken and toss over the heat for about 2 minutes, making sure that they are thoroughly coated with the paste.

3 Add the remaining coconut milk, the chicken stock, and from the tare ingredients, the fish sauce, soy sauce and seasoning to taste. Bring to a simmering point, stirring frequently, then lower the heat and cook gently for 7–10 minutes. Remove from the heat and stir in lime juice to taste.

4 Meanwhile, deep-fry the noodle nests. Two-thirds fill a heavy pan suitable for deep-frying or a deep-fat fryer with oil and heat to 180°C/350°F. Carefully lower in the noodle nests using a slotted spoon and fry briefly, until they turn golden. You may need to do this in batches. Scoop the nests out on to kitchen paper and set aside to drain.

5 Put the ramen noodles in a pan of boiling water and cook for 2–3 minutes or according to packet instructions, until cooked, then remove with a slotted spoon and divide them up between the serving bowls.

6 Divide the chunks of spicy chicken among the bowls and ladle in the hot coconuty chicken broth. Top each serving with chopped spring onions, chillies, shallots, pickled mustard leaves, fried garlic, and finally a fried noodle nest. Garnish with fresh coriander, and serve immediately.

Miso ramen-style chicken soup

Serves 4 | 20 minutes, plus 15 minutes marinating | cook 15 minutes

Udon is a type of chunky white wheat noodle eaten with various hot and cold soups in Japan, but you can swap in standard ramen noodles. In this dish, known as miso nikomi udon, the noodles are cooked in a clay pot with a rich miso soup, chicken, deep-fried tofu and mushrooms before being topped off with a coddled egg.

For the base
900ml/1½ pints/3¾ cups kombu
   dashi stock (see page 12)
300g/10½oz dried udon noodles or
   ramen noodles

For the tare
30ml/2 tbsp mirin
about 90g/3½oz red miso

For the toppings
200g/7oz chicken breast, skin
   removed
10ml/2 tsp sake
2 deep-fried tofu (abura-age)
6 large fresh shiitake mushrooms,
   stalks removed and quartered
4 spring onions/scallions, trimmed
   and chopped into 3mm/⅛in lengths
4 eggs
Japanese spice (shichimi togarashi)
   (optional)

1 First, prepare the toppings. Cut the chicken into bitesize pieces. Sprinkle with sake and leave it to marinate for 15 minutes.

2 Put the tofu in a sieve or strainer and thoroughly rinse with hot water to wash off its oil. Drain on kitchen paper and cut each tofu into four squares.

3 To make the base broth, heat the kombu dashi stock in a large pan. When it has come to the boil, add the chicken pieces, shiitake mushrooms and tofu squares, and cook for 5 minutes. Remove the pan from the heat and add the spring onions.

4 Put the noodles in a pan of boiling water and cook according to packet instructions, about 6–8 minutes for dried or 2–3 minutes for fresh, until they are cooked. Drain the ramen noodles or, if using udon noodles, drain and rinse with cold water to remove any excess starch.

5 Put the tare ingredients into a small bowl. Scoop 30ml/2 tbsp broth from the pan and mix this in well. Mix this taro paste back into the chicken broth and put the pan back over a medium heat; check the taste, adding more miso if required.

6 When the broth has reheated to a bubble, break in the eggs carefully, wait for 1 minute, then cover the pan and remove from the heat. Leave to stand for 2 minutes to coddle the eggs.

7 Divide the noodles among the individual serving pots or bowls. Ladle in the broth to cover the noodles, and arrange the broth ingredients on top – the chicken pieces, tofu, mushrooms and spring onions, carefully adding a coddled egg to each bowl. Serve with a sprinkle of shichimi togarashi, if you like.

Canton-style 'ramen'

Serves 4 | prep 20 minutes | cook 15 minutes

Consisting of a mixture of chicken, prawns, mushrooms and, of course, noodles – which are all cooked in the broth – this is more substantial than some other types of ramen, providing a nutritious meal-in-a-bowl. Hailing from Canton via the Philippines, this is traditionally made with egg noodles but ramen noodles work just as well.

For the base
350ml/12fl oz/scant 1½ cups
   chicken stock (see page 11)
275g/10oz ramen or egg noodles

For the tare
30ml/2 tbsp dark soy sauce

For the toppings
30ml/2 tbsp vegetable oil
3 garlic cloves, peeled and crushed
½ large onion, sliced
250g/9oz shelled prawns/shrimp
1 chicken breast, skin removed and
   sliced into thin strips
4 dried Chinese mushrooms, soaked
   until soft and sliced thinly
40g/1½oz mangetouts/snowpeas
100g/3½oz pak choi/bok choy, sliced
2 fresh red chillies, finely sliced

1 First, prepare the toppings. Heat the oil in a wok or heavy pan over a medium heat and fry the garlic until it is light brown, stirring constantly to prevent it from burning.

2 Add the sliced onion and stir until soft, but not coloured – about 5 minutes. Add the prawns, chicken, mushrooms, mangetouts and pak choi and stir for 2 minutes.

3 Add the chicken stock to the wok or pan along with the soy sauce for the tare and bring to the boil. Add the noodles and cook for 2–3 minutes or according to packet instructions, until tender but not too soft.

4 Divide the mixture between serving bowls and serve garnished with finely sliced red chillies.

Shredded chicken and kimchi ramen

Serves 4 | prep 20 minutes | cook 30 minutes

This nourishing Korean-inspired ramen dish features succulent poached chicken in a light miso broth, with beansprouts for texture and kimchi for heat.

For the base
1.75 litres/3 pints/7½ cups chicken stock (see page 11)
400g/14oz fresh ramen noodles

For the tare
15ml/1 tbsp red miso
15ml/1 tbsp white miso
15ml/1 tbsp light soy sauce
15ml/1 tbsp mirin
15ml/1 tbsp rice vinegar

For the chicken
3–4 chicken breasts
1 lemon grass stalk, trimmed and squashed to bruise
salt and ground black pepper

For the toppings
large handful of beansprouts
30–45ml/2–3 tbsp white cabbage kimchi or kimchi of your choice
10ml/2 tsp black sesame seeds

1 First, cook the chicken. Put 500ml/17fl oz of the chicken stock base in a large pan, add the chicken breasts and lemon grass, and season with salt and pepper. Simmer for 15–20 minutes, until the chicken is cooked through. Pierce with a knife to test: the juices should run clear. If not, cook the chicken for a little longer. Lift out the chicken with a slotted spoon and set it aside on a plate to rest for 5 minutes or so, then tear the chicken into strips and put to one side.

2 Add the rest of the chicken stock to the pan, and heat. Mix together the ingredients for the tare, then whisk them into the broth and bring to the boil. Reduce the heat to a simmer and cook for about 10 minutes.

3 Put the noodles in a pan of boiling water and cook for 2–3 minutes or according to packet instructions, until cooked, then remove with a slotted spoon and divide them between the serving bowls.

4 Ladle over the broth and top with the shredded chicken, beansprouts and kimchi, and sprinkle over black sesame seeds to serve.

Roast duck ramen with pak choi

Serves 6 | prep 30 minutes | cook 3–4 hours

This Chinese-inspired duck and noodle broth makes a delicious meal for colder days. It can be made with leftover roasted duck meat and ready-prepared stock, or by roasting a duck, saving the meat for the soup, and then using the carcass to make the stock.

For the base
1 chicken or duck carcass
2 carrots, peeled and quartered
2 onions, peeled and quartered
4cm/1½in fresh root ginger, peeled and cut into chunks
2 lemon grass stalks, chopped
2.5 litres/4½ pints/10¼ cups water
600g/1lb 6oz fresh ramen noodles

For the tare
30ml/2 tbsp fish sauce (nuoc mam)
15ml/1 tbsp soy sauce
6 black peppercorns

For the duck
225g/8oz roast duck, finely sliced
5ml/1 tsp sunflower oil
2 shallots, finely sliced
4cm/1½in piece of fresh root ginger, peeled and sliced
15ml/1 tbsp soy sauce
10ml/2 tsp sugar
5ml/1 tsp five-spice powder
salt, to taste

For the toppings
175g/6oz pak choi/bok choy
4 spring onions/scallions, sliced
1–2 red and/or green chillies, finely sliced

1 To make the base stock, put the carcass into a deep pan. Add the carrots, onions, ginger, lemon grass, water and the tare ingredients. Bring to the boil and boil for a few minutes, skim off any foam, then reduce the heat and simmer gently with the lid on for 2–3 hours. Remove the lid and continue to simmer for a further 30 minutes to reduce the stock.

2 Skim off any fat, season with salt, then strain the stock. Measure out 2 litres/3½ pints/8½ cups.

3 To prepare the duck, heat the oil in a wok or deep pan and stir in the shallots and ginger, soy sauce, sugar and five-spice powder. Add the measured-out stock and bring to the boil. Season with a little salt, reduce the heat and simmer for 15 minutes.

4 Meanwhile, cut the pak choi into wide strips and blanch in boiling water to soften them. Drain and refresh under cold running water to prevent them cooking any further.

5 Put the noodles in a pan of boiling water and cook for 2–3 minutes or according to packet instructions, until cooked, then remove with a slotted spoon and divide them up between the serving bowls.

6 Lay some of the pak choi and sliced duck over the noodles, then ladle over generous amounts of the simmering broth. Garnish with the spring onions and chillies, and serve immediately.

Fish and Shellfish

Miso salmon and pak choi ramen

Serves 4 | prep 20 minutes | cook 30 minutes

Light, salty kombu dashi stock makes the perfect base for this fish ramen, allowing the flavour of the succulent salmon to dominate, but the richness of which is cut by piquant chilli and aromatic fresh ginger.

For the base
1.75 litres/3 pints/7½ cups kombu
   dashi stock (see page 12)
400g/14oz fresh ramen noodles

For the tare
15ml/1 tbsp white miso
15ml/1 tbsp red miso
15ml/1 tbsp mirin
10ml/2 tsp tahini
pinch of salt

For the miso salmon
4 salmon fillets
15ml/1 tbsp red miso
7.5ml/2½ tsp sesame oil
pinch of ground black pepper

For the toppings
1 bulb of pak choi/bok choy, trimmed
   and leaves separated
1 clump of enoki mushrooms,
   trimmed and separated
30ml/2 tbsp pickled ginger (gari)
1 fresh red chilli, finely sliced
drizzle of sesame oil

1   First, prepare the salmon. Preheat the oven to 190°C/375°F/ Gas 5. Mix the miso and sesame oil together, season the salmon with pepper and coat it with the miso mixture. Place the salmon in a roasting pan and cook for 10–15 minutes, until opaque and cooked through. Remove from the oven and put to one side.

2   Put the stock in a large pan. Mix together the tare ingredients, add to the stock and bring to the boil. Reduce to a simmer, cook for 5 minutes, then taste and add more seasoning if necessary.

3   Cook the pak choi in a pan of boiling salted water for a couple of minutes, then remove with a slotted spoon. Rinse in cold water to prevent further cooking and drain.

4   Add the noodles to the boiling water and cook for 2–3 minutes or according to packet instructions, until cooked, then remove with a slotted spoon and divide them up between the serving bowls.

5   Ladle over the hot broth. Break up the salmon into chunky pieces and add to the bowls along with pak choi, enoki mushrooms, pickled ginger and chilli, and drizzle over a little sesame oil.

Fresh crab and lemon ramen

Serves 4 | prep 20 minutes | cook 20 minutes

Sweet crab tops a light and fragrant lemon grass broth in this fresh-tasting ramen dish. Golden nuggets of corn complement the crab and other flavours perfectly, as well as adding visual and textural interest – which is why corn features in so many different ramen dishes.

For the base
1.75 litres/3 pints/7½ cups kombu dashi or vegetable stock (see pages 11–12)
400g/14oz fresh ramen noodles

For the tare
30ml/2 tbsp light soy sauce
15ml/1 tbsp rice vinegar
15ml/1 tbsp mirin
15ml/1 tbsp sake
10cm/4in piece of fresh root ginger, peeled and finely sliced
1 lemon grass stalk, trimmed and flattened to bruise

For the toppings
300g/10½oz/scant 2 cups corn
about 400g/14oz cooked fresh white crab
2–3 spring onions/scallions, green parts only, finely chopped
large handful of beansprouts
about 6 radishes, finely sliced
30ml/2 tbsp pickled bamboo shoots (menma)
4 lemon slices
pinch of Japanese chilli (nanami togarashi) or dried chilli flakes

1 Put the stock in a large pan. Mix together the tare ingredients, add to the stock and bring to the boil. Reduce to a simmer, cook for 5–10 minutes, then taste and add more seasoning if necessary.

2 Put the noodles in a pan of boiling water and cook for 2–3 minutes or according to packet instructions, until cooked, then remove with a slotted spoon and divide them up between the serving bowls.

3 Add the corn kernels to the hot broth to heat through, then remove with a slotted spoon and spoon them over the noodles.

4 Ladle over the hot stock, then top with crab meat, spring onions, beansprouts, radishes and pickled bamboo shoots. Garnish with lemon slices and sprinkle over the chilli, then serve.

COOK'S TIP: Butter is often added to the top of a hot ramen so it melts in – a little would be delicious over the corn.

Korean-style ramen with fishcake and tofu

Serves 3 | prep 20 minutes | cook 30 minutes

Sold by mobile vendors on bustling street corners, these noodles are a popular and filling snack. Korean fishcake, a processed blend of fish, potato starch and vegetables, is usually found in flat slabs but other shapes, such as balls, are available too. This light, nourishing dish is quick and easy to prepare at home.

For the base
2 litres/3½ pints/8½ cups water
1 sheet of nori, broken into pieces
50g/2oz white radish (daikon), chopped
10g/¼oz dried anchovies
1 leek, sliced
3 garlic cloves, peeled
½ white onion, sliced
300g/10½oz fresh thin wheat noodles (somen) or ramen noodles

For the tare
30ml/2 tbsp dark soy sauce
salt and ground black pepper, to taste

For the toppings
150g/5oz fishcake, sliced, or fish balls
2 sheets dried tofu (yuba), sliced
1 sheet of nori, shredded (optional)
2 spring onions/scallions, shredded
5ml/1 tsp sesame seeds, toasted
5ml/1 tsp Korean chilli powder or flakes

1 First, make the stock for the base. Bring the water to the boil in a large pan. Add the nori, daikon, anchovies, leek, garlic and onion. Bring back to the boil, reduce the heat slightly and boil the stock steadily for 15 minutes.

2 Strain the stock, discarding the flavouring ingredients, then add the soy sauce for the tare, and taste and season as required with salt and pepper.

3 Put the noodles in a pan of boiling water and cook for 1 minute for somen noodles or 2–3 minutes for ramen noodles, or according to packet instructions, until cooked. Remove with a slotted spoon and divide them up between the serving bowls.

4 Bring the broth to the boil. Add the fishcake or fish balls and dried tofu. Boil for 10 minutes, until the tofu is tender.

5 Pour the broth over the noodles in the bowls. Garnish with the nori, if using, and spring onion shreds, and the sesame seeds, then sprinkle with chilli powder before serving.

Variation Fresh tofu can be used as an alternative to dried tofu, but it should not be boiled for 10 minutes. At step 4, add the fishcake or fish balls and simmer for 5 minutes, then add the fresh tofu in one piece and simmer for a further 5 minutes. Use a large spatula or flat draining spoon to lift the tofu carefully from the broth. Slice it and divide it among the bowls, adding it to the noodles. Then pour in the broth. This way the tofu will not disintegrate.

Fresh scallop and bacon ramen

Serves 4 | prep 20 minutes | cook 30 minutes

Salty bacon is a common topping on ramen dishes and here it complements sweet scallops perfectly; the duo are a regular pairing. The remaining ingredients are subtle in order to avoid overpowering the delicate flavour of the scallops.

For the base
1.75 litres/3 pints/7½ cups kombu dashi or vegetable stock (see pages 11–12)
400g/14oz fresh ramen noodles

For the tare
30ml/2 tbsp light soy sauce
15ml/1 tbsp sake
10ml/2 tsp black rice vinegar
pinch of salt

For the toppings
8 streaky bacon rashers/fatty bacon strips
15ml/1 tbsp sunflower oil
12 scallops
2–3 spring onions/scallions, green and white parts separated, finely chopped
5–10ml/1–2 tsp black sesame seeds
handful of fresh coriander/cilantro leaves (optional)

1 First, cook the bacon. Preheat a grill or broiler to high, lay the bacon on the rack and cook until golden and crispy. Remove and put to one side.

2 Heat the oil in a large frying pan or skillet over a high heat until sizzling, then add the scallops and cook for 1–2 minutes per side, until just pale golden. Remove the pan from the heat and put to one side.

3 Put the stock in a large pan. Mix together the tare ingredients, add to the stock and bring to the boil. Reduce to a simmer, cook for 5 minutes, then taste and add more seasoning if necessary.

4 Put the noodles in a pan of boiling water and cook for 2–3 minutes or according to packet instructions, until cooked, then remove with a slotted spoon and divide them up between the serving bowls.

5 Ladle over the hot broth, then top with the scallops and bacon. Add the chopped spring onions and scatter over the black sesame seeds. Garnish with fresh coriander if you like.

COOK'S TIP: You could poach the scallops if preferred – simply add them to the bubbling broth and cook for about 2–3 minutes or until the scallops are cooked through.

Prawn tom yum ramen

Serves 4 | prep 15 minutes | cook 20 minutes

Based on the famous Thai soup, this ramen dish has as its base an intense spicy and sour broth that takes your tastebuds on a real adventure. The soup is topped with fiery prawns to add yet more heat, but soothed by unctuous marinated soft-boiled egg and a tangle of slippery noodles.

For the base
1.75 litres/3 pints/7½ cups kombu dashi or vegetable stock (see pages 11–12)
400g/14oz fresh ramen noodles

For the tare
30ml/2 tbsp light soy sauce
30ml/2 tbsp mirin
15ml/1 tbsp rice vinegar
10–15ml/2–3 tsp tom yum paste (depending on how hot you like it)
pinch of salt

For the spicy prawns
drizzle of sesame oil
300g/10½oz king prawns/jumbo shrimp, shelled
pinch of salt
pinch of ground black pepper
1 fresh red chilli, seeded and finely chopped
5cm/2in piece of fresh root ginger, peeled and grated
2 garlic cloves, peeled and finely chopped

For the toppings
4 marinated soft-boiled eggs (see page 17), halved
large handful of fresh coriander/ cilantro leaves
2–3 spring onions/scallions, green parts only, finely chopped
pinch of Japanese chilli (nanami togarashi) or dried chilli flakes (optional)

1 First, cook the prawns. Heat the sesame oil in a large frying pan, add the prawns, season with salt and pepper and add the chilli, ginger and garlic. Cook for a few minutes, until the prawns are pink and cooked through. Remove from the heat and put to one side.

2 Put the stock in a large pan. Mix together the tare ingredients, add to the stock and bring to the boil. Reduce to a simmer, cook for 5 minutes, then taste and add more seasoning if necessary.

3 Put the noodles in a pan of boiling water and cook for 2–3 minutes or according to packet instructions, until cooked, then remove with a slotted spoon and divide them up between the serving bowls.

4 Ladle over the hot broth and add the prawns. Top with an egg, fresh coriander and spring onions, and sprinkle over the chilli pepper, if using, to serve.

Soba noodles in hot broth with tempura prawns

Serves 4 | prep 20 minutes | cook 30 minutes

Soba noodles are made with buckwheat, which gives them a distinctive nutty and slightly chewy texture that contrasts pleasingly with the crisp lightness of the tempura prawns in this dish. Soba make a good substitute for ramen noodles if you are gluten-intolerant, or simply want to ring the changes.

For the base
900ml/1½ pints/3¾ cups water
900ml/1½ pints/3¾ cups kombu dashi stock (see page 12)
400g/14oz fresh soba noodles or ramen noodles

For the tare
150ml/¼ pint/⅔ cup mirin
150ml/¼ pint/⅔ cup dark soy sauce
25g/1oz dried bonito flakes (kezuri-bushi)
15ml/1 tbsp caster/superfine sugar
5ml/1 tsp salt

For the tempura prawns
16 medium raw tiger or king prawns/jumbo shrimp, heads and shell removed, tails intact
400ml/14fl oz/1⅔ cups ice-cold water
1 large egg, beaten
200g/7oz/scant 2 cups plain/all-purpose flour
vegetable oil, for deep-frying

For the toppings
1 spring onion/scallion, sliced
Japanese spice (shichimi togarashi) (optional)

1. To make the base broth, put the mirin from the tare in a large pan. Bring to the boil, then add the measured water and the remaining tare ingredients. Bring back to the boil, then reduce the heat to low. Skim off any scum that rises and cook for 2 minutes.

2. Strain the broth and put into a clean pan with the dashi stock. Bring to a simmer and keep warm until ready to use.

3. To prepare the prawns, remove the veins that run along their backs using the tip of a sharp knife, then make five shallow cuts into each prawn's belly. Clip the tip of the tail with scissors and squeeze out any moisture from the tail.

4. To make the tempura batter, pour the ice-cold water into a bowl and mix in the beaten egg. Sift in the flour and stir briefly; it should remain fairly lumpy.

5. Heat the oil in a wok or deep-fryer to 180°C/350°F. Hold the tail of a prawn, dunk it in the batter, then plunge it into the hot oil. Deep-fry two prawns at a time until crisp and golden. Drain on kitchen paper and keep warm.

6. Put the noodles in a pan of boiling water and cook for 5–8 minutes if using soba (stirring frequently) or 2–3 minutes if using ramen, or according to packet instructions, until cooked.

7. Tip the soba noodles into a sieve or strainer and wash under cold water, then return them to the pan of broth to heat through before removing with a slotted spoon and dividing them between the serving bowls. For ramen, simply drain and divide them up.

8. Pour the broth over the noodles and place the tempura on top. Sprinkle with spring onion slices and some shichimi togarashi, if you like. Serve immediately.

Mackerel and spring greens ramen

Serves 4 | prep 20 minutes, plus 12 hours steeping | cook 40 minutes

This traditional Japanese broth consists of nutritious smoked mackerel and vibrant spring greens in a wholesome seaweed stock. It differs slightly from other ramens in that the toppings are cooked in with the broth for the last minute, rather than being served on top of the noodles.

For the base
1 x 30cm/12in piece of dried or fresh kombu
750ml/1¼ pints/3 cups water
5 strands of dried or fresh sea spaghetti
smoked mackerel skin
400g/14oz fresh ramen noodles

For the tare
25ml/1½ tbsp rice wine vinegar
1.25cm/½in piece of fresh root ginger, peeled and finely chopped
½ fresh red chilli, finely chopped

For the toppings
200g/7oz spring greens, shredded
1 small leek, finely shredded
1 red bell pepper, finely shredded
200g/7oz smoked mackerel
handful of seaweed, such as dulse flakes (optional)

1 Make the base. If you are using dried kombu, place it in a pan and cover it with water. Bring to the boil, then drain the seaweed in a strainer, discarding the cooking water. This is not necessary if you are using fresh kombu.

2 Pour the fresh measured water into the pan, then add the kombu, sea spaghetti and mackerel skin. Simmer for 20 minutes. Remove the pan from the heat and allow the stock to cool. Transfer it to a bowl, cover and place in the fridge to steep for at least 12 hours.

3 Strain the stock, removing any fat from the surface with a teaspoon or a piece of dried bread, so you are left with a clear, flavoursome stock.

4 Pour the strained stock into a pan, bring it to a simmer and add the spring greens, leek and red pepper. Simmer for 2–3 minutes.

5 Add the tare ingredients and then the smoked mackerel, and simmer for 5 minutes.

6 Add the noodles and cook for 2–3 minutes or according to packet instructions, until cooked. Add the seaweed, if using, to the stock for the last minute to cook through as well.

7 Transfer the noodles, the stock and its contents to serving bowls and serve immediately.

Fresh clam ramen

Serves 4 | prep 30 minutes | cook 20 minutes

The experience of chowing down on salty clams slurped with silky noodles and a tasty hot broth is divine. The subtle and sweet flavour of wakame sea vegetables makes them a fabulous topping that marries well with the more assertive spring onions, pickled ginger and fresh chilli. You'll need napkins at the ready!

For the base
1.75 litres/3 pints/7½ cups kombu dashi or vegetable stock (see pages 11–12)
400g/14oz fresh ramen noodles

For the tare
15ml/1 tbsp light soy sauce
15ml/1 tbsp mirin
15ml/1 tbsp sake (optional)
5ml/1 tsp dark soy sauce
5cm/2in piece of fresh root ginger, peeled and grated
2 garlic cloves, peeled and grated
pinch of sugar
pinch of salt, to taste

For the clams
about 1.2kg/2½lb fresh clams, rinsed (discard any that are open)

For the toppings
handful of shiitake mushrooms, large ones halved
about 30ml/2 tbsp dried wakame, soaked in warm water until reconstituted
30ml/2 tbsp pickled ginger (gari)
2–3 spring onions/scallions, curled (see Cook's Tip)
1 fresh red chilli, finely sliced
few fresh micro or regular coriander/cilantro leaves (optional)

1 Put the stock in a large pan. Mix together the tare ingredients, add to the stock and bring to the boil. Reduce to a simmer, cook for 5 minutes, then taste and add more seasoning if necessary.

2 Pour a small amount of water into the bottom of a wide, shallow pan. Add the clams in a single layer (work in batches if necessary rather than heaping them on top of each other) and steam for about 4 minutes or until they are all open, discarding any that remain shut.

3 Put the noodles in a pan of boiling water and cook for 2–3 minutes or according to packet instructions, until cooked, then remove with a slotted spoon and divide them up between the serving bowls.

4 Ladle over the piping-hot broth. Top with the clams, mushrooms, drained wakame, pickled ginger, spring onion curls, chilli slices and fresh coriander leaves, and serve.

COOK'S TIP: To curl spring onions, first trim the top and bottom, then finely slice lengthways and put them in cold water until they curl.

Spicy mixed seafood ramen

Serves 2 | prep 45 minutes | cook 20–25 minutes

Jjampong is a spicy, garlic-infused seafood stew that makes a real statement for a special occasion. Thick Japanese udon noodles or ramen noodles are added to a rich broth, which is flavoured with characteristically Korean seasonings.

For the base
750ml/1¼ pints/3 cups pork stock
  (see page 10) or other stock
200g/7oz fresh udon or ramen
  noodles

For the tare
1 dried chilli, shredded
2 garlic cloves, peeled and finely
  sliced
5ml/1 tsp grated fresh root ginger
30ml/2 tbsp Korean chilli powder
5ml/1 tsp mirin or rice wine
light soy sauce, to taste
salt, to taste

For the mixed seafood
50g/2oz pork loin
50g/2oz mussels, cleaned (discard
  any that do not open)
50g/2oz prawns/shrimp
90g/3½oz squid, cleaned
15ml/1 tbsp vegetable oil
½ leek, sliced
50g/2oz bamboo shoots, sliced
½ onion, peeled and roughly chopped
50g/2oz carrot, peeled and roughly
  chopped
2 Chinese leaves/Chinese cabbage,
  roughly chopped

1 Slice the pork thinly, put it on a plate and set aside. Prepare the seafood: clean the mussels, peel and devein the prawns, and slice the squid into 2cm/¾in pieces.

2 Coat a large saucepan or wok with the vegetable oil and place over a high heat. When hot, put in the sliced leek and add the sliced dried chilli, garlic and ginger from the tare. Stir-fry until the garlic has lightly browned, then add the sliced pork. Stir-fry quickly.

3 Add the chilli powder and mirin or rice wine from the tare and stir to coat all the ingredients thoroughly.

4 Add the sliced bamboo shoots, onion and carrot, and stir-fry until soft, a few minutes. Add the seafood and cabbage and cook over a high heat for 30 seconds.

5 Pour in the stock and bring to the boil. Reduce the heat. Season with the tare soy sauce and salt to taste, then cover and simmer for 3 minutes. Take off the heat, and discard any closed mussels.

6 Put the noodles in a pan of boiling water and cook for 2–3 minutes or according to packet instructions, until cooked. Remove the ramen noodles, if using, with a slotted spoon and divide them up between the serving bowls; if using udon noodles, drain and rinse them with cold water to remove excess starch, then reheat with hot water and divide them up between the serving bowls.

7 Ladle the broth over the noodles, dividing the seafood and pork evenly among the bowls, and serve.

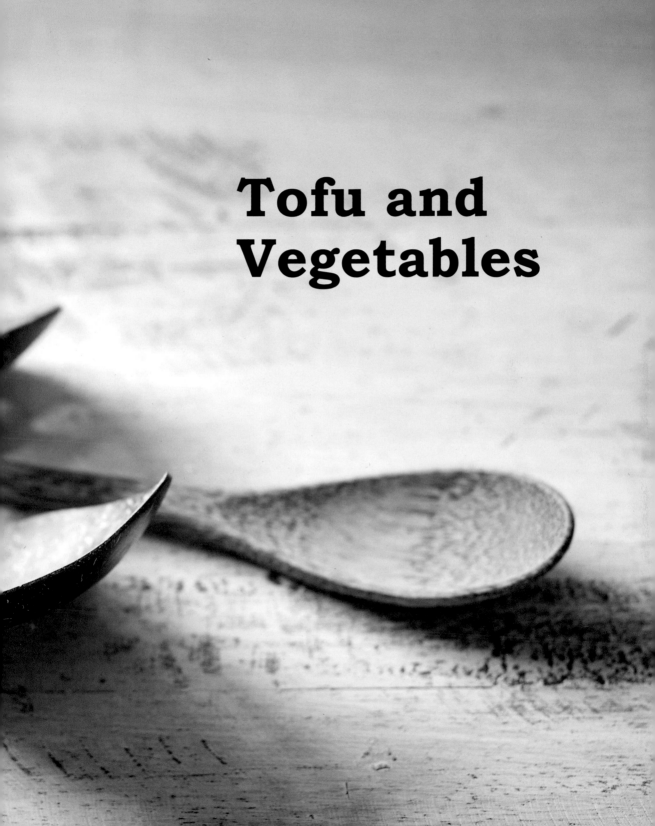

Tofu and Vegetables

Marinated tofu and egg ramen

Serves 4 | prep 15 minutes | cook 30 minutes

This pure-tasting ramen bowl consists of a base with toppings that are simple but well flavoured – a pinch of nanami togarashi or sansyo will liven it all up.

For the base
1.75 litres/3 pints/7½ cups kombu dashi or vegetable stock (see pages 11–12)
400g/14oz fresh ramen noodles

For the tare
30ml/2 tbsp dark soy sauce, or to taste
15ml/1 tbsp mirin
15ml/1 tbsp rice vinegar
5cm/2in piece of fresh root ginger, peeled and finely sliced
½ lemon grass stalk, sliced lengthways

For the marinated tofu
400g/14oz firm tofu, chopped into bitesize pieces
15ml/1 tbsp dark soy sauce
5ml/1 tsp clear honey
5ml/1 tsp mirin
salt and ground black pepper, to taste
30–45ml/2–3 tbsp sesame oil

For the toppings
4 marinated soft-boiled eggs (see page 17), halved
2 sheets of nori, torn into pieces
handful of chives, finely chopped
10ml/2 tsp white sesame seeds
pinch of Japanese chilli (nanami togarashi) or Japanese pepper (sansyo)

1 First, prepare the tofu. Mix together the soy sauce, honey and mirin and season with salt and pepper. Add the tofu pieces and toss to coat.

2 Heat a little of the sesame oil in a wok or frying pan and, when hot, add a few pieces of tofu at time. Cook until golden, then turn and cook the other side. Remove to a plate and repeat the process with the rest of the tofu, adding more oil as required. Put to one side.

3 Put the stock in a large pan. Mix together the tare ingredients, add to the stock and bring to the boil. Reduce to a simmer, cook for 10 minutes, then taste and add more soy sauce if necessary.

4 Put the noodles in a pan of boiling water and cook for 2–3 minutes or according to packet instructions, until cooked, then remove with a slotted spoon and divide them up between the serving bowls.

5 Ladle over the hot stock, top with tofu, marinated eggs and nori seaweed, and sprinkle over chives, sesame seeds and Japanese chilli or pepper to serve.

Teriyaki tofu and spinach ramen

Serves 4 | prep 15 minutes | cook 30 minutes

The tofu provides plenty of protein and texture in this ramen dish and is gently complemented by the delicate and light broth. A last-minute dash of sriracha hot chilli sauce adds a zap of heat, but you could omit it if you prefer.

For the base
1.75 litres/3 pints/7½ cups kombu dashi or vegetable stock (see pages 11–12)
400g/14oz fresh ramen noodles

For the tare
30ml/2 tbsp light soy sauce
15ml/1 tbsp mirin
15ml/1 tbsp rice vinegar
5cm/2in piece of fresh root ginger, peeled and grated

For the teriyaki tofu
about 600g/1lb 6oz tofu, sliced into strips
60–75ml/4–5 tbsp teriyaki sauce
60ml/4 tbsp sesame oil
salt and ground black pepper, to taste

For the toppings
200g/7oz spinach leaves
2 red bell peppers, seeded and chopped into strips
2–3 spring onions/scallions, green parts only, finely sliced
sriracha hot chilli sauce, to serve

1 First, prepare the tofu. Mix together the teriyaki sauce with 15ml/1 tbsp of the sesame oil and season with salt and pepper in a bowl, then add the tofu and gently turn to coat.

2 Heat a little of the remaining sesame oil in a wok or frying pan and, when hot, add a few pieces of tofu at time. Cook until golden, then turn and cook the other side. Remove to a plate and repeat the process with the rest of the tofu, adding more oil as required. Put to one side.

3 Put the stock in a large pan. Mix together the tare ingredients, add to the stock and bring to the boil. Reduce to a simmer, cook for 10 minutes, then taste and add more soy sauce if necessary.

4 Put the noodles in a pan of boiling water and cook for 2–3 minutes or according to packet instructions, until cooked, then remove with a slotted spoon and divide them up between the serving bowls.

5 Ladle over the hot stock and top with the tofu and spinach, pushing it into the stock so it starts to wilt. Add the pepper slices, spring onions and a drizzle of sriracha sauce to serve.

Tofu ramen with peanuts

Serves 4 | prep 20 minutes | cook 20 minutes

This aromatic, spicy ramen dish is an excellent pick-me-up and is packed with protein from the tofu and the roasted peanuts, the latter also adding crunch. As with all ramen recipes, you can adapt the levels of spice and seasoning to suit your palate.

For the base
1 litre/1¾ pints/4 cups vegetable stock (see page 11)
150g/5oz dried thick wheat noodles or ramen noodles

For the tare
15ml/1 tbsp light soy sauce
10ml/2 tsp sugar
5ml/1 tsp finely sliced garlic
5ml/1 tsp finely chopped fresh root ginger
juice of ½ lemon
1 fresh red chilli, seeded and finely sliced

For the toppings
200g/7oz firm tofu
90g/3½oz/scant 1 cup beansprouts
50g/2oz/½ cup peanuts
15ml/1 tbsp chopped fresh coriander/cilantro
1–2 spring onions/scallions, finely sliced into slivers
1 fresh red chilli, seeded and sliced

1 Spread out the noodles out in a shallow dish and pour over boiling water to cover. Soak for 4–5 minutes or until they are just tender (they will be cooked more later, in the broth). Drain, rinse and set aside.

2 Meanwhile, put the stock and all the tare ingredients in a wok or large pan over high heat. Bring to the boil, cover, reduce to a low heat and simmer the mixture gently for 10–12 minutes.

3 Cut the tofu into cubes. Add it to the broth with the drained noodles and the beansprouts. Cook the mixture gently for a further 2–3 minutes.

4 Roast the peanuts in a dry non-stick wok or frying pan, then chop them.

5 Stir the fresh coriander into the broth, then ladle it into serving bowls and serve topped with peanuts, slivers of spring onions and red chilli.

Asparagus, mixed sea vegetable and tofu ramen

Serves 4 | prep 20 minutes | cook 30–40 minutes

Griddling the asparagus adds a smoky sweetness to them, which tastes wonderful with this creamy broth, made with soy milk and earthy seaweed.

For the base
1.75 litres/3 pints/7½ cups kombu dashi stock (see page 12)
400g/14oz fresh ramen noodles

For the tare
300ml/½ pint/1¼ cups soy milk
30ml/2 tbsp light soy sauce
15ml/1 tbsp mirin
salt and ground black pepper, to taste

For the tofu and asparagus
400g/14oz firm tofu, cubed
5ml/1 tsp dark soy sauce
30ml/2 tbsp sesame oil
400g/14oz fine asparagus spears, trimmed

For the toppings
10g/½oz wakame, soaked in water to reconstitute
2 sheets of nori, broken into pieces
2–3 spring onions/scallions, green parts only, finely chopped
10ml/2 tsp black sesame seeds

1 Put the stock in a large pan. Mix together the tare ingredients, add to the stock and bring to the boil. Reduce to a simmer, cook for 15 minutes, then taste and add more seasoning if necessary.

2 Meanwhile, prepare the tofu. Put the tofu in a bowl and toss it in the soy sauce. Heat a little of the sesame oil in a wok or frying pan and, when hot, add a few pieces of tofu at time. Cook until golden, then turn and cook the other side. Remove to a plate and repeat the process with the rest of the tofu, adding a little more oil as required. Put to one side.

3 Heat a griddle pan to hot. Toss the asparagus with the remaining 15ml/1 tbsp sesame oil and add them to the hot pan – you may need to add in batches. Cook for a few minutes or until charred lines appear, then turn and cook the other side for the same time. Put to one side.

4 Put the noodles in a pan of boiling water and cook for 2–3 minutes or according to packet instructions, until cooked, then remove with a slotted spoon and divide them up between the serving bowls.

5 Ladle over the stock, then top with tofu and asparagus. Drain the wakame and divide it up between the bowls, then add the nori and spring onions and sprinkle with the black sesame seeds to serve.

Porcini and sea spaghetti ramen

Serves 4 | prep 10 minutes | cook 35 minutes

The woody, smoky flavour of the porcini mushrooms is complemented by the strong and almost beefy taste of the sea spaghetti to make an intense broth, perfect with noodles for a simple and earthy ramen dish.

For the base
1 litre/1¾ pints/4 cups water
400g/14oz fresh ramen noodles

For the tare
15ml/1 tbsp light soy sauce
15ml/1 tbsp mirin
5ml/1 tsp dark soy sauce

For the mushrooms and sea spaghetti
5g/⅛oz dried porcini mushrooms
20g/¾oz fresh sea spaghetti or
    5g/⅛oz dried sea spaghetti,
    roughly chopped
1 bay leaf
5 spring onions/scallions, sliced

1 Put the measured water in a pan over a medium heat and bring to the boil. Add the mushrooms, sea spaghetti and bay leaf, and simmer for 30 minutes; the smell of wild mushrooms will fill the house!

2 Add the spring onions and all the tare ingredients. Reduce to a simmer, cook for 3 minutes, then taste and add more tare seasonings if necessary.

3 Put the noodles in a pan of boiling water and cook for 2–3 minutes or according to packet instructions, until cooked, then remove and divide between the serving bowls.

4 Pour over the broth, with the mushrooms and sea spaghetti, and serve hot.

Roasted squash and mushroom ramen

Serves 4 | prep 20 minutes | cook 40 minutes

The earthy flavour of mushrooms provides the perfect foil for the soft sweetness of caramelised roasted squash in this delicious autumnal ramen dish, which is jazzed up with a hint of spice from chilli flakes and lent umami depth by miso.

For the base
1.75 litres/3 pints/7½ cups vegetable
   stock (see page 11)
400g/14oz fresh ramen noodles

For the tare
30ml/2 tbsp white miso
30ml/2 tbsp mirin
15ml/1 tbsp rice vinegar

For the roasted squash
1 butternut squash, peeled, halved,
   seeds removed and flesh cubed
15ml/1 tbsp olive oil
pinch each of salt, ground black
   pepper, and dried chilli flakes

For the toppings
200g/7oz chestnut mushrooms,
   sliced
2–3 spring onions/scallions, green
   parts only, finely sliced
1 fresh red chilli, finely sliced
10ml/2 tsp black sesame seeds,
   toasted
handful of purple shiso or Thai basil
   leaves

1 First, prepare the roasted squash. Preheat the oven to 200°C/400°F/Gas 6. Put the squash in a large roasting pan, add the olive oil, season with salt and pepper and add the chilli flakes. Toss together using your hands. Put in the oven and cook for 30–35 minutes or until the squash is golden and tender.

2 Meanwhile, put the stock in a large pan. Mix together the tare ingredients, add to the stock and bring to the boil. Reduce to a simmer, cook for 5 minutes, then taste and add more seasoning if necessary.

3 Put the noodles in a pan of boiling water and cook for 2–3 minutes or according to packet instructions, until cooked, then remove with a slotted spoon and divide them up between the serving bowls.

4 Ladle over the broth, then add the squash to the bowls and top with mushrooms, spring onions, chillies and shiso leaves. Sprinkle over toasted sesame seeds and serve.

COOK'S TIP: You could add the mushrooms to the roasting pan for the last 15 minutes of cooking, which will result in a richer taste.

Curried mixed mushroom ramen

Serves 4 | prep 20 minutes | cook 20 minutes

Mushrooms add a real 'meatiness' to this dish, while the fragrant Japanese curry paste stirred into the stock helps to create a super-rich and tasty broth base.

For the base
1.75 litres/3 pints/7½ cups vegetable stock (see page 11)
400g/14oz fresh ramen noodles

For the tare
15–30ml/1–2 tbsp Japanese curry paste
15ml/1 tbsp dark soy sauce

For the curried mushrooms
15ml/1 tbsp sesame oil
300g/10½oz/4 cups shiitake mushrooms, large ones halved
15ml/1 tbsp Japanese curry paste, mixed with 15ml/1 tbsp water
1 clump of enoki mushrooms, trimmed and roughly separated

For the toppings
2–3 spring onions/scallions, white parts only, finely sliced
1–2 fresh red chillies, seeded and finely sliced
fresh coriander/cilantro leaves, to garnish
5ml/1 tsp white sesame seeds

1 First, prepare the curried mushrooms. Heat the oil in a frying pan or skillet, add the shiitake mushrooms and cook for a minute, then stir in the curry paste and cook for a further minute. Add the enoki mushrooms and stir around the pan until coated. Remove from the heat and put to one side.

2 Put the stock in a large pan. Mix together the tare ingredients, add to the stock and bring to the boil. Reduce to a simmer, cook for 5–10 minutes, then taste and add more soy if necessary.

3 Put the noodles in a pan of boiling water and cook for 2–3 minutes or according to packet instructions, until cooked, then remove with a slotted spoon and divide them up between the serving bowls.

4 Ladle over the broth and top with mushrooms, spring onions, chillies, sesame seeds and fresh coriander to serve.

Shiitake miso ramen

Serves 4 | prep 20 minutes | cook 15 minutes

This delicate, fragrant all-in-one ramen dish is flavoured with just a hint of chilli, allowing the subtle taste of the mushrooms and vegetables to take centre stage. Light and refreshing, it contains fewer noodles than some ramen, but you can always increase the quantity if you want a more substantial dish.

For the base
1 litre/1¾ pints/4 cups water
45ml/3 tbsp barley miso (mugi)
200g/7oz udon noodles, soba
  noodles or Chinese noodles

For the tare
45ml/3 tbsp dark soy sauce
30ml/2 tbsp sake or dry sherry
15ml/1 tbsp rice or wine vinegar
salt and ground black pepper, to taste

For the toppings
115g/4oz asparagus tips or
  mangetouts/snow peas, finely
  sliced diagonally
50g/2oz shiitake mushrooms, stalks
  removed and finely sliced
1 carrot, peeled and sliced into
  julienne strips
3 spring onions/scallions, finely
  sliced diagonally
5ml/1 tsp dried chilli flakes, to serve

1 Put the measured water in a pan and bring to the boil. Measure out 150ml/¼ pint/⅔ cup of this boiling water into a heatproof bowl, then add the miso and stir until dissolved. Set aside.

2 Meanwhile, put the noodles in a pan of boiling water and cook for 4–6 minutes or according to packet instructions, until cooked. Drain the noodles in a colander, rinse under cold running water, then drain again. Set aside.

3 Add the tare ingredients to the pan of boiling water. Boil gently for 3 minutes or until the alcohol has evaporated, then reduce the heat and stir in the miso mixture. Season to taste.

4 Add the asparagus or mangetouts, mushrooms, carrot and spring onions, and simmer for 2 minutes, until the vegetables are tender.

5 Divide the noodles among warm bowls and pour the broth and contents over the top. Sprinkle with the chilli flakes to serve.

COOK'S TIPS:
• Mugi miso is the fermented paste of soybeans and barley.
• If fresh shiitake mushrooms are not available, use dried ones instead. Put them in a bowl, pour over boiling water and leave to stand for 30 minutes.

Griddled courgette and corn ramen with tahini

Serves 4 | prep 20 minutes | cook 30 minutes

Tahini and soya milk are used to flavour the stock in this unusual fusion ramen dish, which results in a rich creamy broth that showcases the vegetable toppings.

For the base
1.75 litres/3 pints/7½ cups kombu dashi or vegetable stock (see pages 11–12)
400g/14oz fresh ramen noodles

For the tare
200ml/7fl oz/scant 1 cup soya milk
15ml/1 tbsp dark soy sauce
15ml/1 tbsp white miso
15ml/1 tbsp tahini

For the griddled courgettes
3 courgettes/zucchini, trimmed and sliced lengthways
drizzle of sesame oil
salt and ground black pepper, to taste

For the toppings
large handful of frozen soya beans, defrosted
300g/10½oz corn, warmed
2–3 spring onions/scallions, green parts only, finely chopped
2 tomatoes, halved, seeded, pulp removed and flesh finely chopped
10ml/2 tsp black sesame seeds
sriracha sauce, to serve

1 First, prepare the courgettes. Heat a griddle pan to hot. In a bowl, toss the courgette slices with the sesame oil and season with salt and pepper. Add a few courgette slices at a time to the hot pan and cook for 2–3 minutes, until charred lines appear on the underside, then turn and cook the other side. Remove to a plate and repeat until all the courgette is cooked. Put to one side.

2 Put the stock in a large pan. Mix together the tare ingredients, add to the stock and bring to the boil. Reduce to a simmer, cook for 10 minutes, then taste and add more seasoning if necessary.

3 Put the soya beans into a large pan of boiling water and cook for about 4 minutes, then remove with a slotted spoon and put to one side.

4 Add the noodles to the pan of boiling water, cook for 2–3 minutes or according to packet instructions, until cooked, then remove with a slotted spoon and divide them up between the serving bowls.

5 Ladle over the hot broth and top with the griddled courgettes, soya beans, corn, spring onions and tomatoes. Sprinkle over the black sesame seeds and a drizzle of sriracha sauce to serve.

Udon noodles with egg broth and ginger

Serves 4 | prep 20 minutes | cook 20 minutes

In this dish, called ankake udon, the broth is thickened with cornflour and retains its heat for a long time. A perfect lunch for a freezing-cold day, it can be made with ramen noodles rather than udon, if you prefer.

For the base
1 litre/1¾ pints/4 cups water
275g/10oz dried udon or ramen
  noodles
30ml/2 tbsp cornflour/cornstarch

For the tare
40g/1½oz kezuri-bushi
25ml/1½ tbsp mirin
25ml/1½ tbsp dark soy sauce
7.5ml/1½ tsp salt

For the toppings
4 eggs, beaten
50g/2oz mustard and cress
2 spring onions/scallions, finely
  chopped
2.5cm/1in piece of fresh root ginger,
  peeled and finely grated

1 To make the base, place the measured water and all the tare ingredients in a pan and bring to the boil on a medium heat. Remove from the heat when it starts boiling. Stand for 1 minute, then strain. Check the taste and add more salt if required.

2 Put the noodles in a pan of boiling water and cook for 6–8 minutes or according to packet instructions, until cooked; if using fresh noodles, cook for less time. Drain the noodles; if using udon noodles, drain and rinse with cold water to remove excess starch. Set aside.

3 Pour the base broth back into a large pan and bring to the boil. Blend the cornflour with 60ml/4 tbsp water. Reduce the heat to medium and gradually add the cornflour mixture to the hot broth. Stir constantly. The broth will thicken after a few minutes. Reduce the heat to low.

4 Mix the eggs, mustard and cress in a small bowl, and stir in the chopped spring onion. Stir the broth once again to create a whirlpool, then pour the egg mixture slowly into the pan.

5 Reheat the noodles if necessary with hot water, then divide them among serving bowls and pour the eggy broth over the top. Garnish with the ginger and serve hot.

COOK'S TIP: Kezuri-bushi is Japanese dried, fermented tuna, found in specialist stores or the Asian aisle in the supermarket.

Sapporo-style miso ramen with sweet-and-sour vegetables

Serves 4 | prep 30 minutes | cook 30 minutes

This ramen features a rich broth base of red miso in which lie noodles topped with crunchy sweet-and-sour veggies and savoury marinated soft-boiled eggs. Delicious.

For the base
1.75 litres/3 pints/7½ cups kombu dashi or vegetable stock (see pages 11–12)
400g/14oz fresh ramen noodles

For the tare
45ml/3 tbsp red miso
15ml/1 tbsp sesame oil
15ml/1 tbsp mirin

For the sweet-and-sour vegetables
drizzle of sesame oil
3–4 carrots, peeled and finely sliced
2–3 spring onions/scallions, trimmed and sliced on the diagonal
30ml/2 tbsp black rice wine vinegar
10ml/2 tsp sugar, or to taste
pinch of dried chilli flakes
2 bulbs of pak choi or choi sum, trimmed and sliced lengthways

For the toppings
large handful of beansprouts
4 marinated soft-boiled eggs (see page 17), halved
10ml/2 tsp black sesame seeds

1 First, prepare the sweet-and sour-vegetables. Heat the oil in a wok, frying pan or skillet, add the sliced carrots and season with salt and pepper. Add the sliced spring onions and toss everything around the pan.

2 Mix the vinegar, sugar and chilli flakes together, raise the heat and add it to the wok. Allow the liquid to bubble, then reduce to a simmer and cook for a few minutes, until the vinegar has evaporated a little. Taste and add more sugar if necessary. Remove from the heat and put to one side. The carrots should still have plenty of crunch.

3 Steam the choi sum in a steamer or in a covered colander set over a pan of simmering water for about 5 minutes, until just tender, then remove and stir into the wok with the carrots, just to coat with a little of the liquid. Put to one side.

4 Meanwhile, put the stock in a large pan. Mix together the tare ingredients, add to the stock and bring to the boil. Reduce to a simmer, cook for 5–10 minutes, then taste and add more seasoning if necessary.

5 Put the noodles in a pan of boiling water and cook for 2–3 minutes or according to packet instructions, until cooked, then remove with a slotted spoon and divide them up between the serving bowls.

6 Ladle over the hot broth, then top with the sweet-and-sour vegetables, the beansprouts and egg, and sprinkle over the black sesame seeds before serving.

COOK'S TIP: For an even more authentic Sapporo ramen add a slice of butter to the top of the steaming-hot dish, as they often do in northern Japan.

Chilled soya milk ramen

Serves 4 | prep 5 minutes, plus overnight soaking and chilling time | cook 5 minutes

Strands of noodles taste great in a mild and deliciously nutty raw chilled broth, making this simple but unusual ramen an ideal dish for a hot summer's day. The iced broth is topped with succulent strips of cucumber and wedges of tomato, reinforcing the sunny nature of the dish.

For the base
30ml/2 tbsp sesame seeds
1 litre/1¾ pints/4 cups water
250ml/8fl oz/1 cup unsweetened
    soya milk
400g/14oz fresh ramen noodles

For the toppings
1 cucumber, cut into thin strips
1 tomato, cut into wedges
salt, to taste

1 Gently toast the sesame seeds in a dry pan until they have lightly browned. Grind them in a blender.

2 Mix the measured water with the soy milk and put in a food processor, then blend with the ground toasted sesame seeds. Pour into a jug or pitcher and refrigerate until well chilled.

3 Put the noodles in a pan of boiling water and cook for 2–3 minutes or according to packet instructions, until cooked, then drain them and rinse them well in cold water.

4 Place a portion of the noodles in each soup bowl and pour over the chilled soya milk broth. Top with strips of cucumber and tomato wedges, then season with salt to taste and serve.

COOK'S TIP: This quick and easy version uses soya milk; for the more authentic but time-consuming technique soak 225g/8oz/1 cup soya beans overnight, rinse and remove the skins, then place with the toasted sesame seeds in a food processor and blend till fine. Then, strain through muslin or cheesecloth, collecting the liquid in a jug or pitcher. Chill the soya-sesame broth in the refrigerator before pouring over the noodles.

Bean, lime and coconut ramen

Serves 4 | prep 15 minutes | cook 30 minutes

The addition of coconut milk is maybe not so authentic but it works as a tasty base from which to slurp the noodles in this ramen. Top with lots of fresh coriander to add flavour and fragrance to the dish.

For the base
1.75 litres/3 pints/7½ cups kombu dashi or vegetable stock (see pages 11–12)
300ml/½ pint/1¼ cups coconut milk
400g/14oz fresh ramen noodles

For the tare
30ml/2 tbsp dark soy
15ml/1 tbsp mirin
juice of ½ lime
pinch of sugar (optional)

For the beans
300g/10½ oz fine green beans
300g/10½ oz soya beans, defrosted if frozen

For the toppings
300g/10½ oz corn
large handful of beansprouts
large handful of fresh coriander/cilantro
lime wedges, to serve
pinch of Japanese chilli (nanami togarashi) or Japanese pepper (sansyo), to serve

1 Put the stock in a large pan. Mix together the tare ingredients, add to the stock along with the coconut milk and bring to the boil. Reduce to a simmer, cook for 10–15 minutes, then taste and add more seasoning if necessary.

2 Meanwhile, put the green beans in a large pan of boiling salted water and cook for about 4 minutes, until just tender but retaining some bite. Remove to a dish with a slotted spoon and set aside. Add the soya beans to the boiling water and cook for 2–3 minutes, then remove with a slotted spoon and put them with the green beans. Warm the corn in the water too for a minute, remove and drain.

3 Add the noodles to the boiling water and cook for 2–3 minutes or according to packet instructions, until cooked, then remove with a slotted spoon and divide them up between the serving bowls.

4 Ladle over the hot broth and top with green beans, soya beans, corn and beansprouts. Add the fresh coriander, lime wedges and a sprinkling of Japanese chilli or pepper to serve.

COOK'S TIP: If you choose to use a low-fat coconut milk, be careful as it will be more prone to splitting.

Nutritional Notes

pork stock (per 1000ml) Energy 80kcal/310kJ; Protein 1g; Carbohydrate 9.7g, of which sugars 1.1g; Fat 4g, of which saturates 1g; Cholesterol 0mg; Calcium 0mg; Fibre 0g; Sodium 0mg.

chicken stock (per 1000ml) Energy 71kcal/297kJ; Protein 4.6g; Carbohydrate 3g, of which sugars 0.6g; Fat 4.6g, of which saturates 0g; Cholesterol 0mg; Calcium 36mg; Fibre 0g; Sodium 0mg.

kombu dashi stock (per 600ml) Energy 48kcal/186kJ; Protein 0.6g; Carbohydrate 5.8g, of which sugars 0.6g; Fat 2.4g, of which saturates 0.6g; Cholesterol 0mg; Calcium 0mg; Fibre 0g; Sodium 0mg.

noodles (per recipe) Energy 1028kcal/4364kJ; Protein 33.4g; Carbohydrate 213.7g, of which sugars 4.1g; Fat 10.3g, of which saturates 2.4g; Cholesterol 231mg; Calcium 419mg; Fibre 11.4g, Sodium 92mg.

marinated soft-boiled egg (serves 4) Energy 95kcal/396kJ; Protein 7.7g; Carbohydrate 0.4g, of which sugars 0.4g; Fat 6.7g, of which saturates 1.9g; Cholesterol 231mg; Calcium 36mg; Fibre 0g; Sodium 440mg.

burned garlic oil (per 50ml) Energy 362kcal/1491kJ; Protein 3.8g; Carbohydrate 7.8g, of which sugars 0.8g; Fat 35.3g, of which saturates 4.1g; Cholesterol 0mg; Calcium 9mg; Fibre 2.6g; Sodium 2mg.

Char siu pork in miso ramen (serves 6) Energy 773kcal/3233kJ; Protein 45.7g; Carbohydrate 53.1g, of which sugars 3.2g; Fat 43.4g, of which saturates 15g; Cholesterol 150mg; Calcium 43mg; Fibre 3.8g; Sodium 455mg.

Smoky pork and bacon ramen (serves 4) Energy 636kcal/2683kJ; Protein 40.4g; Carbohydrate 79.6g, of which sugars 9.3g; Fat 19.6g, of which saturates 5.9g; Cholesterol 106mg; Calcium 105mg; Fibre 7.3g; Sodium 1473mg.

Sapporo-style ramen noodles in broth (serves 4) Energy 207kcal/863kJ; Protein 12.1g; Carbohydrate 12.5g, of which sugars 5.8g; Fat 10.2g, of which saturates 2.5g; Cholesterol 19mg; Calcium 71mg; Fibre 3.6g; Sodium 1390mg.

Tokyo-style ramen noodles in broth (serves 4) Energy 676kcal/2850kJ; Protein 44.6g; Carbohydrate 74.6g, of which sugars 4.5g; Fat 22.2g, of which saturates 5.7g; Cholesterol 224mg; Calcium 69mg; Fibre 4.8g; Sodium 2173mg.

Spicy curried minced pork ramen (serves 4) Energy 746kcal/3134kJ; Protein 46.5g; Carbohydrate 74.6g, of which sugars 2.9g; Fat 31g, of which saturates 9.1g; Cholesterol 344mg; Calcium 150mg; Fibre 5.1g; Sodium 731mg.

Thai-style pork and peanut ramen (serves 4) Energy 659kcal/2777kJ; Protein 41.6g; Carbohydrate 79g, of which sugars 5.2g; Fat 21.8g, of which saturates 5.4g; Cholesterol 93mg; Calcium 92mg; Fibre 6.1g; Sodium 1478mg.

Pork and mushroom ramen (serves 4) Energy 775kcal/3263kJ; Protein 62.1g; Carbohydrate 73.2g, of which sugars 3.1g; Fat 29.4g, of which saturates 7.5g; Cholesterol 371mg; Calcium 111mg; Fibre 6.8g; Sodium 715mg.

Tonkotsu ramen with braised pork (serves 4–6) Energy 604kcal/2533kJ; Protein 33.5g;

Carbohydrate 49.8g, of which sugars 3g; Fat 30.4g, of which saturates 10.1g; Cholesterol 245mg; Calcium 58mg; Fibre 3.3g; Sodium 1494mg.

Shoyu beef and chinese leaf ramen (serves 4) Energy 581kcal/2451kJ; Protein 35.3g, Carbohydrate 74.2g, of which sugars 4.2g; Fat 17.9g, of which saturates 4.8g; Cholesterol 89mg; Calcium 66mg; Fibre 4.8g; Sodium 1579mg.

Cold beef broth with buckwheat ramen (serves 4) Energy 431kcal/1816kJ; Protein 24.1g; Carbohydrate 62.1g, of which sugars 18.1g; Fat 11.2g, of which saturates 3.3g; Cholesterol 163mg; Calcium 65mg; Fibre 5.4g; Sodium 267mg.

Teriyaki beef ramen with pickled vegetables (serves 4) Energy 649kcal/2735kJ; Protein 39.5g; Carbohydrate 82.9g, of which sugars 10.7g; Fat 18.6g, of which saturates 4.5g; Cholesterol 88mg; Calcium 117mg; Fibre 8.4g; Sodium 1343mg.

Beef ramen with oyster mushrooms (serves 2) Energy 776kcal/3252kJ; Protein 32.1g; Carbohydrate 82.8g, of which sugars 4g; Fat 37.4g, of which saturates 7.6g; Cholesterol 287mg; Calcium 100mg; Fibre 5.8g; Sodium 1382mg.

Miso steak and tomato ramen (serves 4) Energy 577kcal/2435kJ; Protein 37g; Carbohydrate 75.5g, of which sugars 2.9g; Fat 16.1g, of which saturates 4.5g; Cholesterol 89mg; Calcium 63mg; Fibre 4.7g; Sodium 675mg.

Vietnamese-style beef ramen (serves 6) Energy 347kcal/1468kJ; Protein 19.8g; Carbohydrate 53.2g, of which sugars 5.2g; Fat 7.7g, of which saturates 2.4g; Cholesterol 41mg; Calcium 56mg; Fibre 4g; Sodium 690mg.

Curried beef ramen (serves 4) Energy 602kcal/2539kJ; Protein 42.2g; Carbohydrate 73.9g, of which sugars 3.4g; Fat 17.3g, of which saturates 4.6g; Cholesterol 103mg; Calcium 114mg; Fibre 4.6g; Sodium 841mg.

Griddled chicken and mushroom ramen (serves 4) Energy 682kcal/2885kJ; Protein 52.4g; Carbohydrate 92g, of which sugars 10.7g; Fat 14.2g, of which saturates 3.3g; Cholesterol 135mg; Calcium 58mg; Fibre 6.3g; Sodium 841mg.

Spicy seasoned chicken and vegetable ramen (serves 4) Energy 796kcal/3330kJ; Protein 32g; Carbohydrate 78.3g, of which sugars 7.4g; Fat 41.5g, of which saturates 8.8g; Cholesterol 113mg; Calcium 166mg; Fibre 7.8g; Sodium 427mg.

Fried chilli chicken ramen (serves 4) Energy 605kcal/2551kJ; Protein 35.1g; Carbohydrate 81.6g, of which sugars 4.8g; Fat 17.6g, of which saturates 3.8g; Cholesterol 96mg; Calcium 41mg; Fibre 4.2g; Sodium 777mg.

Fiery chicken ramen-style with crispy noodles (serves 4) Energy 802kcal/3376kJ; Protein 41.9g; Carbohydrate 112.6g, of which sugars 11.4g; Fat 22.2g, of which saturates 4.6g; Cholesterol 161mg; Calcium 128mg; Fibre 4.6g; Sodium 1488mg.

Miso ramen-style chicken soup (serves 4) Energy 816kcal/3423kJ; Protein 61.6g; Carbohydrate 62g, of which sugars 2.9g; Fat 37.1g, of which saturates 3.8g; Cholesterol 289mg; Calcium 1930mg; Fibre 3.5g; Sodium 1087mg.

Canton-style 'ramen' (serves 4) Energy 423kcal/1783kJ; Protein 28.5g; Carbohydrate 53.2g, of which sugars 4.3g; Fat 12.1g, of which saturates 2.4g; Cholesterol 164mg; Calcium 126mg; Fibre 4.3g; Sodium 832mg.

Shredded chicken and kimchi ramen (serves 4) Energy 530kcal/2243kJ; Protein 36.9g; Carbohydrate 74.8g, of which sugars 2.7g; Fat 11.3g, of which saturates 2.9g; Cholesterol 96mg; Calcium 61mg; Fibre 4.6g; Sodium 779mg.

Roast duck ramen with pak choi (serves 6) Energy 476kcal/2012kJ; Protein 21.3g; Carbohydrate 76.4g, of which sugars 5.7g; Fat 11.5g, of which saturates 3.1g; Cholesterol 71mg; Calcium 138mg; Fibre 5g; Sodium 918mg.

Miso salmon and pak choi ramen (serves 4) Energy 662kcal/2784kJ; Protein 40.1g; Carbohydrate 74g, of which sugars 2.3g; Fat 24.8g, of which saturates 5g; Cholesterol 93mg; Calcium 104mg; Fibre 5g; Sodium 547mg.

Fresh crab and lemon ramen (serves 4) Energy 544kcal/2295kJ; Protein 33g; Carbohydrate 74.9g, of which sugars 3.4g; Fat 14g, of which saturates 3.1g; Cholesterol 102mg; Calcium 38mg; Fibre 4.7g; Sodium 1136mg.

Korean-style ramen with fishcake and tofu (serves 3) Energy 493kcal/2085kJ; Protein 17.2g; Carbohydrate 86.8g, of which sugars 3.7g; Fat 10.9g, of which saturates 2.7g; Cholesterol 42mg; Calcium 63mg; Fibre 5g; Sodium 1025mg.

Fresh scallop and bacon ramen (serves 4) Energy 593kcal/2498kJ; Protein 31.8g; Carbohydrate 74.6g, of which sugars 2.7g; Fat 20.7g, of which saturates 5.7g; Cholesterol 79mg; Calcium 68mg; Fibre 4.3g; Sodium 1217mg.

Prawn tom yum ramen (serves 4) Energy 547kcal/2306kJ; Protein 33.6g; Carbohydrate 72.8g, of which sugars 2.8g; Fat 15.5g, of which saturates 4.3g; Cholesterol 407mg; Calcium 144mg; Fibre 3.9g; Sodium 947mg.

Soba noodles in hot broth with tempura prawns (serves 4) Energy 676kcal/2851kJ; Protein 25g; Carbohydrate 102.4g, of which sugars 3.8g; Fat 21.3g, of which saturates 4.1g; Cholesterol 159mg; Calcium 124mg; Fibre 5.4g; Sodium 1612mg.

Mackerel and spring greens ramen (serves 4) Energy 608kcal/2556kJ; Protein 23.9g; Carbohydrate 76.8g, of which sugars 6.5g; Fat 24.5g, of which saturates 5.6g; Cholesterol 83mg; Calcium 153mg; Fibre 7.8g; Sodium 568mg.

Fresh clam ramen (serves 4) Energy 466kcal/1971kJ; Protein 26.9g; Carbohydrate 74.1g, of which sugars 2.5g; Fat 8.9g, of which saturates 2.5g; Cholesterol 89mg; Calcium 98mg; Fibre 4.4g; Sodium 1588mg.

Spicy mixed seafood ramen (serves 2) Energy 588kcal/2479kJ; Protein 34.4g; Carbohydrate 82.5g, of which sugars 10g; Fat 18.9g, of which saturates 3.7g; Cholesterol 200mg; Calcium 162mg; Fibre 8.9g; Sodium 484mg.

Marinated tofu and egg ramen (serves 4) Energy 634kcal/2666kJ; Protein 30.3g; Carbohydrate 74g, of which sugars 3.7g; Fat 26.2g, of which saturates 5.8g; Cholesterol 261mg; Calcium 618mg; Fibre 7.8g; Sodium 852mg.

Teriyaki tofu and spinach ramen (serves 4) Energy 546kcal/2301kJ; Protein 26.1g; Carbohydrate 81.7g, of which sugars 8.5g; Fat 14.9g, of which saturates 3.2g; Cholesterol 30mg; Calcium 808mg; Fibre 5.9g; Sodium 1348mg.

Tofu ramen with peanuts (serves 4) Energy 262kcal/1103kJ; Protein 12.6g; Carbohydrate 29.9g, of which sugars 2.4g; Fat 11.1g, of which saturates 2.2g; Cholesterol 11mg; Calcium 281mg; Fibre 2.1g; Sodium 72mg.

Asparagus, mixed sea vegetable and tofu ramen (serves 4) Energy 611kcal/2570kJ; Protein 30g; Carbohydrate 76.2g, of which sugars 5.6g; Fat 22.8g, of which saturates 4.5g; Cholesterol 30mg; Calcium 675mg; Fibre 14.6g; Sodium 933mg.

Porcini and sea spaghetti ramen (serves 4) Energy 400kcal/1693kJ; Protein 13.2g; Carbohydrate 72.6g, of which sugars 2.7g; Fat 8.4g, of which saturates 2.3g; Cholesterol 30mg; Calcium 40mg; Fibre 5.1g; Sodium 548mg.

Roasted squash and mushroom ramen (serves 4) Energy 499kcal/2112kJ; Protein 16g; Carbohydrate 84.3g, of which sugars 7.9g; Fat 13.3g, of which saturates 3g; Cholesterol 30mg; Calcium 116mg; Fibre 7.7g; Sodium 462mg.

Curried mixed mushroom ramen (serves 4) Energy 478kcal/2016kJ; Protein 12.6g; Carbohydrate 72.6g, of which sugars 2.5g; Fat 17.3g, of which saturates 3.4g; Cholesterol 30mg; Calcium 41mg; Fibre 3.9g; Sodium 562mg.

Shiitake miso ramen (serves 4) Energy 250kcal/1056kJ; Protein 9.1g; Carbohydrate 44.6g, of which sugars 4.8g; Fat 4.2g, of which saturates 0.1g; Cholesterol 0mg; Calcium 40mg; Fibre 3.7g; Sodium 1221mg.

Griddled courgette and corn ramen with tahini (serves 4) Energy 576kcal/2430kJ; Protein 22.7g; Carbohydrate 90.3g, of which sugars 7.5g; Fat 16.2g, of which saturates 3.5g; Cholesterol 30mg; Calcium 132mg; Fibre 9.8g; Sodium 607mg.

Udon noodles with egg broth and ginger (serves 4) Energy 418kcal/1765kJ; Protein 21.7g; Carbohydrate 60g, of which sugars 2.3g; Fat 11.4g, of which saturates 2g; Cholesterol 282mg; Calcium 181mg; Fibre 3g; Sodium 970mg.

Sapporo-style miso ramen with sweet-and-sour vegetables (serves 4) Energy 585kcal/2464kJ; Protein 23.6g; Carbohydrate 81.6g, of which sugars 8.5g; Fat 20.4g, of which saturates 5g; Cholesterol 261mg; Calcium 175mg; Fibre 8g; Sodium 748mg.

Chilled soya milk ramen (serves 4) Energy 458kcal/1934kJ; Protein 15.3g; Carbohydrate 73.1g, of which sugars 3.1g; Fat 13.7g, of which saturates 3.3g; Cholesterol 30mg; Calcium 92mg; Fibre 5.5g; Sodium 204mg.

Bean, lime and coconut ramen (serves 4) Energy 616kcal/2605kJ; Protein 28.3g; Carbohydrate 96.4g, of which sugars 11.8g; Fat 15.9g, of which saturates 3.4g; Cholesterol 30mg; Calcium 168mg; Fibre 14.2g; Sodium 805mg.

Index

This edition is published by Lorenz Books
an imprint of Anness Publishing Ltd
www.annesspublishing.com
info@anness.com

© Anness Publishing Ltd 2024

A CIP catalogue record for this book is available from the British Library.

Although the advice and information in this book are believed to be accurate at the time of going to press, neither the author nor the publisher can accept any legal responsibility or liability for any errors or omissions that may have been made nor for any inaccuracies nor for any loss, harm or injury that comes about from following instructions or advice in this book.

Publisher: Joanna Lorenz
Special photography: William Shaw
Special food styling: Heather Whinney
With thanks to the additional contributors.
Design: Adelle Mahoney
Editorial: Lucy Doncaster
Nutritional consultant: Clare Emery
Thanks to shutterstock (page 9)
and istock (page 22)

COOK'S NOTES
Bracketed terms are intended for American readers. For all recipes, quantities are given in both metric and imperial measures and, where appropriate, in standard cups and spoons. Follow one set of measures, but not a mixture, because they are not interchangeable.

Standard spoon and cup measures are level. 1 tsp = 5ml, 1 tbsp = 15ml, 1 cup = 250ml/8fl oz.

Australian standard tablespoons are 20ml. Australian readers should use 3 tsp in place of 1 tbsp for measuring small quantities.

American pints are 16fl oz/2 cups. American readers should use 20floz/2½ cups in place of 1 pint when measuring liquids.

A drizzle is approximately ½–1 tbsp; a pinch is approximately ¼ tsp.

Since ovens vary, you should check with your manufacturer's instruction book for guidance.

The nutritional analysis given for each recipe is calculated per portion (i.e. serving or item), unless otherwise stated. If the recipe gives a range, such as Serves 4–6, then the nutritional analysis will be for the smaller portion size, i.e. 6 servings. The analysis does not include optional ingredients, such as salt added to taste.